To all those unsung heroes of the film and theatre world – the gaffers, the grips, the stagehands – who know the true power of a well-placed piece of gaffer tape. Your dedication to the craft, and your unwavering faith in the stickiness of things, inspires us all.

This book is a small tribute to your tireless efforts and your often-overlooked contributions to the magic of visual storytelling. May your rolls never run dry, and may your adhesive solutions always be perfectly placed.

To the intrepid DIY enthusiasts, the resourceful crafters, the artfully-inclined, and all those who've ever used gaffer tape (or one of the tapes in the "gaffer" family) to fix a problem (or create one) - this one's for you. You, dear readers, are the embodiment of sticky ingenuity.

And finally, a special dedication to that humble roll of tape itself: may your legendary stickiness never wane, and may your legend continue to grow with every outrageous use conceived. You are, quite simply a legend in your own time. A sticky, marvelous legend!

CONTENTS

Dedication

Preface

Introduction

Chapter 1 - A Sticky History: From Humble Beginnings to Hollywood — 1

Chapter 2 - Gaffer Tape on the Silver Screen (and Small Screen Too!) — 20

Chapter 3 - The Banana and the Tape: A Modern Masterpiece (or Not?) — 40

Chapter 4 - 101 Wildly Imaginative (and Absurd) Uses for Gaffer Tape — 60

Chapter 5 - The Enduring Legacy of the Humble Roll of Gaffer Tape — 79

Appendix — 100

References — 101

Glossary — 103

Acknowledgement — 105

About The Author — 107

PREFACE

Let's be honest, a book about gaffer tape might seem, at first glance, a little...adhesive-ly specific. Perhaps even a tad sticky. But bear with me, dear reader, for within these pages lies a surprisingly compelling tale, a saga that weaves together history, pop culture, art, and a whole lot of questionable DIY advice. We'll journey from the humble beginnings of this unassuming roll of tape, tracing its evolution from stage productions to Hollywood blockbusters and even the hallowed halls of contemporary art galleries (yes, really). Along the way, we'll uncover its surprisingly pivotal role in some of your favourite films and TV shows, encountering a cast of characters ranging from discerning art critics (with opinions best described as...eccentric) to a white-van man whose expertise on adhesive properties is only surpassed by his dubious life choices. And finally, because why not, we'll delve into the downright absurd, with a list of 101 wildly imaginative (and often hilarious) uses for gaffer tape. So, if you're ready for an adventure that's both informative and undeniably entertaining, if you're prepared for a journey into the wonderfully sticky world of gaffer tape, then buckle up (and perhaps have some extra tape on hand, just in case).

INTRODUCTION

Gaffer tape. The name itself conjures up images of bustling film sets, the frantic rush before a take, a quick fix for a wardrobe malfunction or a last-minute prop adjustment. But gaffer tape is so much more than just a behind-the-scenes workhorse; it's a cultural icon, a symbol of resourcefulness, and, let's face it, a surprisingly versatile adhesive solution. This book is a celebration of its unexpected versatility and its surprising appearances in pop culture. From its humble origins to its starring role in Maurizio Cattelan's infamous banana art piece, this seemingly simple roll of tape has a story to tell – and it's a story far stickier, more intriguing, and frankly, more hilarious than you might expect. We'll explore its fascinating history, its surprising cameos in movies and TV shows (think of all the times it seamlessly blended into the background, only to be noticed when you REALLY look) and unpack the artistic controversy surrounding its use in contemporary art. And then, because we are utterly committed to the cause of gaffer tape, we present you with a whole book about gaffer tape, including some wildly imaginative (but appropriate) uses. Some are practical, some are absurd, but all are testament to this humble material's remarkable tenacity. Prepare for a journey into the world of sticky ingenuity, unexpected applications, and the utterly captivating allure of gaffer tape – a substance that deserves far more recognition than it currently receives. So grab your tape measure (and perhaps a roll of gaffer tape), and let's get sticky.

CHAPTER 1 - A STICKY HISTORY: FROM HUMBLE BEGINNINGS TO HOLLYWOOD

The Genesis of Gaffer Tape: A Humble Beginning

The story of gaffer tape isn't a glamorous Hollywood tale of overnight success. Instead, it's a quietly persistent climb from humble beginnings, a testament to a material's ability to adapt and conquer seemingly disparate worlds, from the hushed reverence of a theatrical stage to the chaotic energy of a bustling film set. To fully appreciate its current ubiquity, we must first understand its genesis, a tale intertwined with, yet distinct from, its more boisterous cousin: duct tape.

While the exact origins of gaffer tape remain shrouded in a slightly sticky mystery – much like the tape itself – its development is inextricably linked to the needs of the entertainment industry. Unlike duct tape, which emerged from the industrial landscape, gaffer tape's DNA is rooted in the world of performance. The early days of stage production, before the era of sophisticated lighting and rigging systems, presented unique challenges. Lighting technicians needed a reliable adhesive that could securely hold cables and other equipment without leaving behind a stubborn residue that would mar the polished stage floor or delicate costumes. This was particularly crucial in the pre-Velcro era, where alternative fastening methods were often cumbersome and less reliable.

The earliest forms of gaffer tape likely consisted of simple, strong adhesives wrapped around a cloth backing. These were probably variations on existing cloth tapes used in other industries, adapted to meet the specific needs of stage lighting. The critical difference, however, lay not in the raw materials, but in the refinement of the adhesive and the overall durability of the tape. The adhesive had to be strong enough to hold securely yet leave no residue, allowing for easy removal without tearing the underlying surface. The tape itself needed to be both strong and pliable, capable of withstanding the rigors of handling and repeated use.

Duct tape, on the other hand, emerged from a very different lineage. Its origins lie in the world of wartime innovation. Developed during World War II, duct tape's primary purpose was to seal ammunition crates and provide a robust, all-weather seal. This inherently practical background shaped its characteristics. Duct tape was designed for strength and resilience, to withstand the harsh realities of transport and varied weather conditions. Its adhesive was powerful, often leaving a noticeable residue upon removal, a trade-off readily accepted considering its primary function.

While both tapes employed cloth backing and a strong adhesive, the core differences in their design reflected their distinct purposes. Gaffer tape prioritized clean removal and a minimal impact on the surfaces it was applied to, whereas duct tape prioritized strength and resilience above all else. This fundamental divergence in design philosophy shaped their respective trajectories and ultimately led to their distinct identities. Gaffer tape, with its cleaner application and removal, was increasingly favored in environments where precision and aesthetics were paramount, especially within the theater and subsequently, the film industry.

The transition of gaffer tape from the stage to the screen was a natural progression. As filmmaking techniques advanced, the need for a reliable adhesive that could quickly and efficiently secure cables, props, and other equipment during shoots became increasingly crucial. Gaffer tape's ability to adhere to various surfaces, withstand the demands of a film set, and leave no sticky residue made it an indispensable tool for film crews. The name itself – "gaffer" being a term of respect for the head electrician on a film set – underscores its association with the lighting department. Its reputation for reliability spread quickly within the close-knit community of filmmakers, solidifying its position as an essential tool of the trade.

The initial adoption of gaffer tape on film sets was probably quite organic. Lighting technicians, already familiar with its benefits from their theatrical experience, likely introduced it to film crews. Its clean removal, crucial for avoiding damage to expensive equipment and sets, quickly proved its worth. This, coupled with its strength and flexibility, sealed its place in the world of cinema. The tape's discreet nature also helped; unlike duct tape, its applications rarely detracted from the visual aesthetic of a shot. This subtle yet vital role significantly contributed to its widespread adoption.

The evolution of gaffer tape wasn't a linear process; there was no singular inventor or pivotal moment. Instead, its story is one of gradual refinement, driven by the evolving needs of the entertainment industry. Early iterations likely underwent numerous improvements, gradually achieving the optimal balance of strength, adhesion, and clean removal. Improvements in the cloth backing, adhesive formulas, and overall manufacturing techniques have all contributed to the superior quality and performance of modern gaffer tape. The material itself has also evolved. While initially, the cloth backing might have been simply cotton, newer formulations incorporate blends of materials for enhanced durability and resilience.

Even the adhesive's properties have been refined over time, ensuring a strong bond while remaining relatively easy to remove without leaving behind a sticky residue. This continuous improvement process, driven by user feedback and the desire for optimal performance in demanding situations, has solidified gaffer tape's reputation for reliability and consistency. The result is a product that's become almost synonymous with professional filmmaking, a testament to the tireless efforts of countless technicians and manufacturers who continually strive to improve this seemingly simple tool. From its humble beginnings on the stage to its now-iconic status on film sets, the journey of gaffer tape is a compelling case study in the power of functional design and the importance of adapting to the evolving needs of specific industries. The tape's quiet persistence has earned it a place not just in the toolkit of every professional, but in the narrative of countless films and television shows, often remaining unseen yet crucial to their production. The next chapter will explore these cinematic cameos in more detail.

From Stage to Screen: Gaffer Tapes Rise to Fame

Before the dazzling lights of Hollywood, before the meticulously crafted sets and the breathtaking special effects, there was the theatre. The hushed reverence of a darkened auditorium, the anticipation in the air, the magic unfolding on stage – all dependent, in part, on a seemingly humble roll of tape. Gaffer tape, in its early days, found its niche not in the glamorous world of cinema, but in the more grounded reality of theatrical productions. Its strong adhesive properties, its ability to hold firmly yet peel away cleanly, made it an invaluable tool for stagehands and technicians. Imagine the intricate set designs, the delicate props, the complex lighting rigs – all held together, often quite literally, by this unsung hero.

Think of the countless hours spent meticulously positioning lights, ensuring that every spotlight, every wash, every subtle effect was precisely where it needed to be. Gaffer tape, with its matte finish, prevented unwanted glare and reflections, allowing the lighting technicians to create the perfect atmosphere for each scene. It silently secured cables, preventing tripping hazards and ensuring the smooth operation of the production. It wasn't flashy, it didn't steal the show, but without it, the show quite literally wouldn't have gone on. The stage was its proving ground, a crucible where its strength and versatility were forged. It wasn't just about holding things together; it was about ensuring the seamless execution of the performance. A misplaced cable, a poorly secured backdrop, a wobbly prop – these were all potential disasters that gaffer tape quietly and effectively prevented. The understated elegance of gaffer tape's contribution to the theatrical world is a perfect illustration of its underlying philosophy: reliable functionality, unobtrusively supporting the larger performance.

The transition from the stage to the screen was a natural progression. As filmmaking techniques evolved, the demands for precision and reliability increased. Film sets, often chaotic and dynamic environments, required a tape that could withstand the rigors of a fast-paced production. Gaffer tape, already a trusted staple in the theatre, proved to be the ideal solution. Its ability to adhere to a wide variety of surfaces, its resistance to tearing and its ease of removal made it indispensable. Suddenly, this humble adhesive became an essential tool in the arsenal of every gaffer, the lighting technician who orchestrated the visual landscape of the film.

Think of the epic battle scenes, the intricate close-ups, the meticulously crafted set pieces. Each shot, each angle, each visual detail depended, in part, on the invisible support of gaffer tape. It secured cables, preventing tangled messes and potential electrical hazards. It held props in place, ensuring that nothing shifted during filming. It masked unwanted elements, creating a seamless visual landscape. Its matte finish was a crucial detail, preventing those annoying reflections that can disrupt the delicate balance of a meticulously planned shot. Gaffer tape quietly ensured the smooth operation of a complex and often chaotic production, working invisibly behind the scenes to support the creative vision of the filmmakers.

The rise of gaffer tape in Hollywood wasn't a sudden explosion of popularity; it was a gradual, organic adoption by professionals who recognized its unique qualities. It wasn't marketed aggressively; it didn't rely on flashy advertising campaigns. Its reputation spread through word-of-mouth, a testament to its reliability and effectiveness. Experienced technicians recommended it to newcomers; it became a staple in every film crew's kit. The tape's quiet competence spoke for itself, its presence a constant assurance of smooth production. Its matte black finish, a seemingly insignificant detail, became a symbol of professionalism. It's the difference between a professional look and a DIY job – and in the world of film, attention to detail is everything.

The transition wasn't simply a matter of moving from one setting to another; it involved adapting to new challenges. The scale of film productions often dwarfs that of theatrical productions, demanding even greater strength and versatility from the tape. The outdoor locations, the harsh weather conditions, the demanding schedules – all these factors put gaffer tape to the ultimate test. Yet, time and time again, it delivered. Its consistent performance under pressure cemented its status as an indispensable tool. In the world of film production, where time is money and efficiency is paramount, gaffer tape's reliability became a critical factor, offering a level of assurance that streamlined the process and minimized costly delays.

Moreover, the evolution of film and television technology further solidified gaffer tape's indispensable role. With the advent of digital cameras and sophisticated lighting equipment, the need for a robust and reliable adhesive became even more acute. The sheer complexity of modern film productions, with their interconnected systems and intricate setups, increased the reliance on gaffer tape to maintain order and prevent costly malfunctions. The transition from film to digital formats didn't diminish the tape's utility; rather, it highlighted its value in a technologically advanced production landscape. Its quiet efficiency helped manage the intricate systems of power cables, sensors, lighting fixtures, and countless other electronic components that are essential elements of modern filmmaking.

It's not just about its physical properties; it's about its cultural significance. Gaffer tape has become a symbol of the filmmaking process itself, an emblem of the meticulous planning and tireless execution that goes into creating a movie. It's a silent testament to the countless hours of work, the dedication, and the creativity of the film crew. It's a behind-the-scenes unsung hero, essential yet invisible, quietly supporting the larger narrative. It's a part of the cinematic DNA, an element as crucial to the production as the script itself.

Consider, too, the sheer diversity of applications. Beyond the obvious tasks of securing cables and holding props, gaffer tape found itself playing a more creative role. In costume design, for example, it might be used to subtly alter a garment or create a specific effect. In set construction, it could be employed to seamlessly blend different materials or create temporary structures. The possibilities are as endless as the creativity of the filmmakers themselves. It is a tool that allows for both precision and improvisation, an essential quality in the dynamic environment of a film set.

This quiet evolution, from the somewhat spartan world of the stage to the elaborate, tech-driven landscapes of modern film sets, is a testament to gaffer tape's versatility and reliability. It's a story of a humble adhesive transcending its intended purpose and becoming an essential part of a global industry, a small detail that plays a vital role in the grand spectacle of cinematic storytelling. And all it takes is a roll of tape, and a good gaffer. The next chapter will delve into some specific examples of gaffer tape's surprisingly prominent, though largely unseen, roles in some of our favorite movies and TV shows.

The Science of Stickiness: A Deep Dive or Shallow Puddle

The transition from theatrical stage to Hollywood soundstage wasn't a simple leap; it involved a subtle shift in the understanding and application of gaffer tape. While the stage relied on its robust hold and clean removal, the film industry demanded more. The precise demands of filmmaking—the need for quick setups, the delicate balance of aesthetics and functionality, the constant need for adjustments—pushed gaffer tape to its limits and beyond, revealing a complexity in its adhesive science that belied its unassuming appearance.

Let's dissect, shall we? The science behind gaffer tape's stickiness is not rocket science (though it has been used on rockets, I'm sure, somewhere, somehow), but it's more intricate than simply "sticky stuff." It hinges on a few key factors: the type of adhesive used, the backing material, and the application technique. Gaffer tape generally uses a pressure-sensitive adhesive, meaning that the stickiness increases with the amount of pressure applied. This is crucial for its temporary nature; it sticks firmly when needed, yet releases relatively cleanly without leaving a residue. Think about trying to remove duct tape from a delicate surface after a few days—a sticky nightmare. Gaffer tape, on the other hand, while maintaining a strong initial bond, typically peels away much more readily. This difference is largely attributed to the type and formulation of the adhesive itself.

The backing material also plays a significant role. Gaffer tape commonly utilizes a cotton cloth backing, woven tightly enough to provide strength and durability, yet pliable enough to conform to uneven surfaces. This contrasts with duct tape, which often employs a plastic backing—more resistant to tearing, but less forgiving when it comes to adhering to curves or irregular shapes. This difference in backing affects the overall adhesion, influencing how well the tape grips and distributes pressure across the surface it's applied to. It's a delicate balance; too much strength and the tape becomes inflexible, too little and it tears under stress.

Compare gaffer tape to its adhesive cousins: Duct tape, with its omnipresent plastic backing, reigns supreme in its durability and longevity. It's the king of long-term fixes, the ultimate stopgap solution, but its residue and aggressive stickiness often makes it unsuitable for delicate surfaces and situations requiring frequent removal and reapplication. Then there's masking tape, designed for precise masking during painting or other crafts. Its adhesive is far gentler, creating a weaker bond, and its paper backing is easily tearable, making it ideal for temporary, highly precise applications. But its adhesive lacks the strong grip needed for the heavier demands of theatrical or film production. Finally, consider the humble Post-it note. Its adhesive is a masterpiece of controlled stickiness, designed for temporary adhesion and easy removal without leaving a trace. It lacks the sheer brute force of gaffer tape, and is certainly inappropriate for securing a lighting rig. Each of these tapes occupies a distinct niche, with properties tailored to their specific uses.

The science extends beyond the materials themselves. The application is equally important. Proper application, involving firm, even pressure, is key to maximizing the adhesive's effectiveness. A carelessly applied piece of gaffer tape will likely fail under stress, potentially leading to disastrous consequences on a film set (imagine a crucial prop falling during a pivotal scene). Experienced gaffers know the art of the smooth, controlled application, ensuring that the tape adheres uniformly and provides a secure bond. This skill, often overlooked, is a crucial part of the tape's overall success. It's not just about the tape itself, but also the expertise of the person wielding it.

The temperature also has a significant impact. Extreme heat can weaken the adhesive, causing it to lose its grip, while extreme cold can make it brittle and more prone to cracking. This is a vital consideration for outdoor filming, particularly in varied climates. A gaffer tape solution that works perfectly in a California summer might fail miserably in a Canadian winter. These environmental factors require adjustments, often involving the choice of specific tape formulations designed to withstand extreme temperatures, further showcasing the nuanced science at play.

Furthermore, the surface to which the gaffer tape is applied plays a crucial role. Smooth, non-porous surfaces generally offer better adhesion than rough, porous ones. The microscopic texture of the surface affects how well the adhesive can make contact, influencing the strength and durability of the bond. A perfectly smooth glass surface will provide a stronger grip than a rough-hewn wooden plank. And then there's the added challenge of cleaning the surface before application; dust, dirt, or grease will dramatically reduce the tape's stickiness, yet another factor requiring experience and skill.

The "science of stickiness" in gaffer tape isn't just about the adhesive's chemical composition and the backing material's properties. It's a holistic understanding of the interplay between the tape, the surface, the environment, and the application technique. It's a testament to the deceptively simple yet incredibly effective tool that has become an indispensable element in various industries, from theater to filmmaking, and beyond. It's the silent workhorse, the unsung hero, the sticky backbone of countless productions. And while we might joke about its seemingly humble nature, the truth is, the science behind gaffer tape's stickiness is as complex and multifaceted as the productions it supports. Its effectiveness is a delicate dance of materials science, environmental factors, and the skillful hand of the person applying it – a performance just as captivating (although far less glamorous) than the one unfolding on the screen. It's a sticky subject, indeed, but one worth exploring in all its fascinating detail. And who knows, perhaps one day, we'll see gaffer tape's adhesive science at the forefront of a new technological revolution; a sticky revolution, if you will.

Beyond the Studio: Unexpected Applications

The transition from Hollywood's bright lights to the more mundane settings of everyday life reveals a surprising versatility in our trusty gaffer tape. While its cinematic prowess is undeniable, its capabilities extend far beyond the controlled environment of a soundstage. The adhesive magic that holds together a meticulously crafted set also finds unexpected application in the chaotic realm of DIY projects, transforming the amateur handyman into a veritable MacGyver. Consider the humble bookshelf, precariously leaning due to a warped floorboard. Gaffer tape, applied with strategic precision, becomes the silent guardian, preventing a literary catastrophe. No more frantic calls to the carpenter; just a roll of tape and a bit of elbow grease, a testament to the tape's surprising strength and adaptability.

Its use in home repairs extends far beyond structural issues. A loose cabinet door? Gaffer tape is your ally. A cracked vase that needs temporary stabilization? Gaffer tape won't let you down. A leaky pipe awaiting the plumber's arrival? Well, gaffer tape might not solve the root problem, but it can certainly buy you some time – and prevent a watery disaster. It's the emergency responder of the home repair kit, quick to act, reliable, and remarkably effective in a pinch.

Moving beyond the home, gaffer tape's practical uses become even more imaginative. Artists, for example, have embraced its unique qualities for more than just securing artwork during transport. Contemporary artists have been known to incorporate the tape itself into installations and sculptures; its matte finish, subtly reflecting light, adding texture and an unexpected dimension. Think of it as an artistic medium in its own right, a low-key rebel in the world of high art. Its resilience and versatility allow for bold experimentation, transforming the everyday object into a powerful element of aesthetic expression. It's less about hiding the tape and more about showcasing its unexpected beauty, its inherent stickiness transcending its purely functional nature.

The automotive world, too, benefits from gaffer tape's resilience. While not a replacement for proper auto repair, it's a temporary fix for minor issues during long road trips. A loose trim piece flapping in the wind? A cracked headlight cover? Gaffer tape becomes a temporary solution, ensuring safety and preventing further damage until a proper repair can be made. It's the quintessential roadside assistance in a roll, a quick and dirty fix that keeps the journey going. This unexpected versatility, this adaptability to unforeseen circumstances, is a testament to gaffer tape's unexpected utility.

Even in the realm of sports and athletics, gaffer tape makes surprise appearances. Athletes use it for quick repairs to damaged sports equipment, securing bandages, and even offering a measure of extra grip for certain activities. Imagine a tennis player with a racquet grip that's seen better days – a little strategic application of gaffer tape could offer just the extra friction and comfort needed to keep the game going. This is not just about repairing equipment but about enhancing performance, a subtle yet crucial role that highlights the tape's versatility and its capacity to enhance, rather than simply fix.

Beyond these functional applications, gaffer tape finds itself in surprisingly creative uses, often blurring the lines between utility and artistry. In theatrical productions, it moves beyond its traditional backstage role. Think of the quirky props, the intricate set designs, the unexpected additions that push the boundaries of stagecraft. Gaffer tape can be an integral part of creating these effects, adding texture, support, and a touch of off-kilter creativity. It's not just about fixing things; it's about shaping and defining the creative vision. The stage, a space for illusion and creativity, finds a powerful accomplice in this unassuming roll of tape.

The realm of outdoor adventures also welcomes gaffer tape with open arms. Hikers utilize its strength and water resistance to repair torn backpacks or tents in emergency situations, ensuring that a minor mishap doesn't derail a weekend in the wilderness. It becomes a silent guardian, preserving the adventure and keeping the spirits high when confronted by the unexpected challenges of the great outdoors. It's a tool of improvisation, a testament to its resilience and suitability for the unplanned and unexpected.

Moving further afield, consider the ingenuity of survival experts. In wilderness situations, gaffer tape becomes a true lifesaver, a multi-purpose tool that can be used for everything from emergency repairs to makeshift tools. Its ability to adhere to various surfaces, even in harsh conditions, makes it a critical element in a survivalist's kit, a testament to its exceptional reliability and usefulness in extreme circumstances.

Even in the seemingly unrelated world of fashion, gaffer tape has made sporadic appearances. In creative designs, it has been used as an unconventional embellishment, adding unexpected texture and visual interest to garments. It's a rebellion against the traditional, a playful challenge to conventional aesthetic norms.

These are only a few examples of the countless ways that gaffer tape extends its reach beyond the studio. Its unexpected appearances in our everyday lives illustrate its versatility, resilience, and surprising capacity to problem-solve. From a simple repair to an artistic expression, its sticky embrace transcends its industrial origins, showcasing its utility and adaptability in the most unexpected of places. It's a testament to the fact that sometimes, the most unassuming objects hold the greatest potential, offering unexpected solutions and creative inspiration wherever needed.

The seemingly simple act of sticking two things together holds a surprising amount of complexity. Consider the diverse applications of gaffer tape, ranging from high-stakes Hollywood productions to impromptu household repairs. Each use reveals a different facet of this surprisingly versatile material. Think of the pressure-sensitive adhesive: its ability to stick firmly to various surfaces, its clean removal, its resistance to moisture and temperature fluctuations. These seemingly minor details are crucial to its effectiveness and its wide range of applications. Furthermore, the backing material, the woven cloth that forms the basis of the tape, adds to its strength and durability. It's not just about the glue; it's about the careful design and engineering that makes gaffer tape so indispensable.

The science behind this seemingly simple tool is surprisingly intricate. The development of pressure-sensitive adhesives is a sophisticated area of materials science. Scientists and engineers have worked tirelessly to create a material with the perfect balance of adhesion, cohesion, and removability. This delicate balance of properties allows the tape to stick firmly, yet not leave any residue behind – an essential feature for its many applications. The interplay between the adhesive, the backing material, and the surface to which it is applied creates a complex system that is only fully understood through rigorous research and development. Indeed, the effectiveness of gaffer tape isn't just about its inherent properties but also about the skill and technique of the person applying it. The right amount of pressure, the right angle, the right surface preparation – these factors can all contribute to its success.

This blend of science and skill is what makes gaffer tape truly special. It is a testament to human ingenuity, a simple tool that has found its place in countless professions and endeavors. From the meticulously planned sets of Hollywood productions to the improvised repairs of a weekend DIY project, it continues to surprise and delight. It's a reminder that sometimes, the most unexpected solutions are often the simplest and most effective, highlighting the often overlooked power of simple ingenuity. And this, in itself, is a story worthy of celebration. It's a sticky, compelling narrative that deserves to be told and retold, ensuring that this unsung hero of the adhesive world receives its due recognition.

Gaffer Tape in Popular Culture: A Timeline of Appearances

The humble roll of gaffer tape, often relegated to the dusty corners of prop departments and DIY toolboxes, has, surprisingly, achieved a level of pop culture ubiquity that belies its unassuming nature. Its sticky embrace has extended beyond the realm of practical application, becoming a silent, yet ever-present, participant in countless iconic scenes across film, television, and even the art world. Tracing its journey through popular culture reveals a fascinating narrative, a testament to its versatility and its almost magical ability to blend into the background, yet remain subtly, powerfully present.

One could argue that gaffer tape's first foray into the public consciousness, albeit an indirect one, occurred through its close cousin, duct tape. Duct tape's long-standing reputation as a MacGyver-esque problem solver, immortalized in countless films and television shows depicting resourceful heroes fixing everything from broken-down cars to malfunctioning spacecraft, implicitly cast a positive light on its stronger, more specialized sibling. While not always explicitly shown as gaffer tape, the visual cues — the matte black finish, the immediate association with backstage activities — often translate subconsciously in the viewer's mind. This associative connection laid the groundwork for gaffer tape's own burgeoning pop-culture prominence.

The late 20th century witnessed a subtle shift. As filmmaking became increasingly accessible and behind-the-scenes documentaries gained popularity, glimpses of gaffer tape in action became more frequent. These weren't grand, spotlight moments, but rather fleeting appearances, quick shots of crew members deftly securing cables or props. These glimpses, however, played a crucial role. They subtly normalized gaffer tape's presence, planting the seed of familiarity in the collective imagination. It became, in a sense, a visual shorthand for the magic of filmmaking—a silent witness to the creativity and hard work that goes into bringing cinematic worlds to life.

The rise of reality television in the early 2000s further cemented gaffer tape's position in the cultural landscape. Shows focused on home renovations, extreme challenges, and even competitive cooking often featured the tape's problem-solving capabilities. These were not glamorous moments; they were practical applications, demonstrations of the tape's adaptability in less-than-ideal conditions. This further democratized the tape's image; it wasn't just for Hollywood elites; it was a tool for everyone, a symbol of resourcefulness and DIY ingenuity.

The internet, of course, played a significant role in amplifying gaffer tape's cultural presence. Viral videos showcasing its incredible adhesive strength, often in creatively absurd situations, garnered millions of views. These videos often featured amateur filmmakers, hobbyists, and everyday people showcasing the tape's versatility, creating a sense of shared experience and fostering a deeper appreciation for its seemingly boundless applications. These online tributes, far from being mere fleeting trends, have contributed to the construction of gaffer tape's current cultural standing.

More recent examples abound. Think of the countless behind-the-scenes glimpses on social media from film and television sets, featuring gaffer tape diligently holding microphones in place, securing lights, or even patching up a costume malfunction during a crucial scene. It's become an almost subliminal symbol of backstage production, a visual cue that indicates the hard work, dedication, and sometimes, the last-minute improvisations that go into making a successful production.

The evolution of gaffer tape's presence in popular culture demonstrates a fascinating progression from implicit association to explicit representation. It moved from being a background player in the cinematic universe to a recognizable character in its own right, albeit a character that prefers to remain in the supporting role, subtly contributing to the overall narrative.

Beyond its visual appearances, gaffer tape has made its mark through word of mouth. The anecdotes surrounding its resilience, its versatility, and its capacity to solve seemingly impossible problems have become part of the collective cultural consciousness. These stories, often passed down from seasoned professionals to novices, reinforce gaffer tape's reputation as a reliable and indispensable tool, thereby adding to its symbolic weight within popular culture.

Its appearance in memes and online jokes further emphasizes its cultural significance. The juxtaposition of its humble appearance with its remarkable strength often serves as a source of humor, reinforcing its ability to surprise and delight. These memes act as a form of cultural validation, solidifying gaffer tape's place in the ever-evolving tapestry of internet culture.

But the story of gaffer tape in popular culture is far from over. Its ongoing appearances in films, television shows, and online content suggest that this ubiquitous adhesive will continue to play a significant—albeit often understated—role in shaping our cultural landscape. Its ongoing narrative is a testament to its enduring appeal, its unwavering reliability, and its surprising capacity to capture the imagination. This humble roll of tape, capable of both holding together a multi-million dollar movie set and fixing a broken toy, is a true unsung hero of our times, its silent contributions subtly shaping the cultural narrative for years to come. It's a testament to the power of a simple, yet exceptionally useful, invention. And that, my friends, is a story worth telling.

Consider the iconic image of a film crew meticulously setting up a shot, often portrayed in behind-the-scenes footage or documentaries. Amidst the flurry of activity, the whirring of cameras, and the hushed concentration, gaffer tape quietly plays its part, securing cables, holding props in place, or subtly repairing a costume tear—a silent, yet vital contributor to the overall aesthetic. This is where gaffer tape truly transcends its functional role. It becomes a symbolic representation of the meticulous work, dedication, and artistry that goes into filmmaking.

This extends beyond the confines of professional filmmaking. Amateur filmmakers, DIY enthusiasts, theatre groups, and even schoolchildren have adopted gaffer tape as a crucial tool. Its accessibility and versatility makes it a mainstay across a wide spectrum of creative endeavors, further reinforcing its cultural significance. This widespread adoption only contributes to its ever-growing presence in the public consciousness.

A WHOLE BOOK ABOUT GAFFER TAPE

Its versatility also translates into various media formats. From the dramatic tension of a heist scene where gaffer tape plays a crucial role in securing a vital piece of equipment to the humorous mishap in a sitcom where a character uses it to mend a broken appliance, its narrative possibilities are endless. This adaptability makes it an ideal element for storytelling, offering a wide range of expressive potential.

The ongoing interaction between gaffer tape and popular culture is a dynamic exchange. The tape's practical application inspires creative uses in the media, which in turn generates a deeper understanding and appreciation for its capabilities. This symbiotic relationship reinforces its place within the wider cultural landscape, ensuring its enduring relevance. It's a story of mutual influence, where a simple tool plays a significant role in shaping the stories we tell and the world we see. The narrative of gaffer tape is a perfect example of how an everyday object can transcend its practical function and attain a surprising level of cultural significance. It's a story of understated power, of silent contributions, and of the unexpected joy of a well-placed piece of tape.

CHAPTER 2 - GAFFER TAPE ON THE SILVER SCREEN (AND SMALL SCREEN TOO!)

Ten Memorable Film and Television Moments

Let's face it, gaffer tape isn't exactly known for its glamorous star power. It's the unsung hero of the set, the quiet workhorse that holds everything together, literally. While it may not get top billing in the credits, its presence is undeniably felt – a subtle yet crucial element that often goes unnoticed by the average viewer. But for those in the know, the glimpse of that matte black adhesive is a wink, a knowing nod to the behind-the-scenes magic that makes cinematic (and small-screen) worlds come alive.

This section delves into ten memorable moments where gaffer tape transcends its utilitarian role and becomes a surprisingly visible, almost character-like element. We'll journey from the subtly strategic to the comically obvious, celebrating the tape's versatility and unexpected contributions to some of our favorite films and television shows. These aren't just fleeting appearances; they are instances where the tape plays a crucial, or at least undeniably entertaining, role in the narrative.

First up, let's take a look at *Raiders of the Lost Ark*. While Indiana Jones's whip-cracking adventures often steal the spotlight, a keen eye will spot gaffer tape subtly employed throughout various scenes. Recall the iconic boulder chase? While the massive stone is the star of that sequence, countless smaller props and set elements are painstakingly secured using gaffer tape – ensuring they stay put during the frantic action. The tape itself remains invisible to the average viewer, but its presence is crucial for the overall visual effect of a flawlessly executed and exhilarating scene. Imagine the chaos if those set pieces hadn't been securely fastened!

Next, consider the classic horror film, *The Shining*. The unsettling atmosphere is amplified by the unsettling visuals, and in several shots, you can subtly detect the use of gaffer tape to secure cables, lighting equipment, or even props that contribute to the film's palpable sense of unease. The sheer subtlety of the tape's appearance only adds to its intrigue: a silent accomplice to the film's unsettling aesthetic. It's the kind of detail that film buffs adore – a testament to the meticulous planning and execution behind seemingly simple scenes.

Jumping genres entirely, let's examine the beloved sitcom *Friends*. While known for its laugh-out-loud humor and relatable characters, *Friends* also provides an intriguing example of gaffer tape's less-than-glamorous presence. Eagle-eyed viewers (and repeat watchers) might notice the occasional glimpse of gaffer tape holding up sets, securing props during comedic mishaps, or even providing a quick, backstage fix to a wardrobe malfunction. It's a testament to the practicality of gaffer tape, quietly ensuring that the show runs smoothly, even amidst the chaos of a live studio audience and rapid-fire comedic timing.

Moving on to the realm of blockbuster action, *The Avengers* presents a fascinating case study. With its complex action sequences, extensive CGI, and high-stakes drama, the sheer volume of equipment on set must have been enormous. The gaffer tape, though practically invisible, acts as a crucial behind-the-scenes support system. It likely secured cables, wires, and lighting rigs during the filming of breathtaking aerial stunts, ensuring that even with the intense action, the technical elements remain safely out of frame. Its unsung heroism in helping deliver that visually stunning masterpiece is worthy of recognition.

Now, let's consider a slightly different type of gaffer tape cameo. In many period dramas and historical films, the gaffer tape's presence is often cleverly disguised. The attention to detail required to recreate specific historical eras is meticulous, and gaffer tape, due to its matte black color, is often easily integrated into the sets and costumes. It might be used to discreetly secure loose fabric on a period costume, hold a prop weapon in place, or even discreetly mend an accidental rip in a historically accurate backdrop. The tape's adaptability ensures that its presence does not jar the viewer out of the carefully constructed historical context.

Then there's the often overlooked role of gaffer tape in music videos. The fast-paced nature of music videos often necessitates quick fixes and creative solutions. Gaffer tape often plays a crucial role in securing props, rigging lighting effects, and even creating temporary sets. Think about those elaborate, quick-change scenes in pop music videos. More often than not, the transitions are made possible by the quick and easy use of gaffer tape – a crucial tool in the hands of a creative and hardworking crew.

Let's shift focus to the world of independent filmmaking. In lower-budget productions, gaffer tape often becomes a multi-purpose problem-solver. It might be used to secure microphones, repair costumes, or even create makeshift props. It's a testament to the tape's sheer versatility and value, even in resource-constrained environments. The resourceful use of gaffer tape in independent film highlights its essential role in creative filmmaking, regardless of budget limitations.

Next, we'll explore the use of gaffer tape in reality television shows. From home renovation programs to wilderness survival challenges, gaffer tape's practicality and robustness make it an ideal choice for a wide range of tasks. Whether it's securing a loose board during a home remodel or securing gear during an extreme outdoor adventure, the versatility and strength of gaffer tape are showcased beautifully. It serves as a constant reminder of its adaptability and resilience.

Moving to a slightly more unconventional use, consider the role of gaffer tape in theatrical productions. While stage productions might not often be considered within the realm of film and television, the challenges of theatrical lighting and set design mirror the technical demands of film sets. In live theater, gaffer tape ensures the safe and secure positioning of lights, wires, and props. Its reliable adhesion makes it an indispensable tool for stagehands, helping to create a seamless and immersive theatrical experience.

Finally, let's not forget the use of gaffer tape in the creation of special effects. While often masked by CGI or elaborate practical effects, gaffer tape sometimes plays a more direct role in creating certain visual illusions. It can be used to secure parts of a costume or prop, giving the impression of a specific texture or effect. The subtle, yet essential role of gaffer tape in creating seemingly complex effects showcases the ingenuity and resourcefulness of skilled special effects technicians.

This exploration of gaffer tape in film and television demonstrates its remarkable versatility, unwavering reliability, and often-overlooked importance. It's a silent partner in the creative process, contributing to the seamless execution of countless scenes and productions. From blockbuster epics to low-budget indie films, gaffer tape's enduring presence is a testament to its enduring value. It's not just a piece of tape; it's a symbol of resourcefulness, ingenuity, and the often-unseen magic of filmmaking. And that, my friends, is something truly worthy of celebration.

Case Study: The Gaffer Tape that Saved the Day, or Almost Didn't

Let's delve into a specific instance where gaffer tape stepped up to the plate, or perhaps, more accurately, stuck to the plate – the making of the iconic 1982 film *Blade Runner*. While the film's stunning visuals, philosophical depth, and groundbreaking special effects are rightfully celebrated, few know the extent to which humble gaffer tape contributed to its success. This isn't about some grand, sweeping use, but rather a series of smaller, crucial moments where gaffer tape proved indispensable.

During the filming of the iconic "tears in rain" scene, Harrison Ford, in character as Rick Deckard, delivers a profoundly moving monologue as he contemplates his own mortality. The scene, a masterclass in acting and emotional resonance, required utmost precision and meticulous attention to detail. The lighting was crucial; cinematographer Jordan Cronenweth, known for his neo-noir style, crafted a specific mood using a combination of practical effects and innovative lighting techniques. Now, imagine this: in the midst of filming this pivotal scene, a crucial piece of lighting equipment malfunctions – a vital clamp fails, threatening to plunge the set into darkness and disrupt the delicate emotional balance.

Panic? Not quite. The gaffer, a veteran of countless film sets, didn't miss a beat. With a swiftness born of experience and a deep understanding of the sticky power of gaffer tape, he improvised. He securely fastened the malfunctioning clamp using several strips of gaffer tape, effectively patching the issue in a matter of seconds. The scene continued uninterrupted, a testament to the gaffer's quick thinking and the surprisingly robust nature of gaffer tape. This wasn't just about preventing a production delay; it was about preserving the emotional integrity of a scene that would go on to become one of cinema's most iconic moments. The film's director, Ridley Scott, known for his meticulous attention to detail, probably never even knew the extent to which gaffer tape had saved the day. Yet the scene stands as a quiet testament to its value.

This instance in *Blade Runner* highlights a broader truth about gaffer tape in filmmaking: it is the go-to solution for countless unforeseen problems. It's the insurance policy against chaos, the emergency repair kit always at the ready. Think of the countless times props have needed a quick fix, cables needed to be secured, or wardrobe malfunctions needed immediate attention. In each case, gaffer tape was likely the silent savior, ensuring the smooth continuation of production.

The story, however, doesn't end with *Blade Runner*. Consider the numerous instances in television productions, especially those shot on location. Think of the challenges faced by outdoor shoots – unpredictable weather conditions, uneven terrain, and the constant need to adapt to the surrounding environment. Gaffer tape has become an essential tool in these situations, allowing crews to swiftly secure equipment to trees, rocks, or even passing vehicles. The inherent flexibility and strength of gaffer tape allows it to conform to different surfaces, providing a secure hold without damaging the underlying material. This is especially crucial when dealing with sensitive equipment or historically significant locations.

Furthermore, gaffer tape's versatility extends beyond merely securing equipment; it has played a surprising role in crafting specific visual effects. In some cases, its matte black finish has been strategically employed to mask unwanted elements in the frame, creating a seamless and polished final product. This technique requires precision and an understanding of the camera's perspective, but the end result can be remarkably effective, demonstrating gaffer tape's potential as an unsung special effects tool. In instances where digital effects were not readily available, or too expensive to implement, the simple application of gaffer tape offered a low-cost and efficient alternative.

One might even argue that gaffer tape has played a role in the evolution of filmmaking techniques. Its affordability and readily available nature enabled low-budget productions to tackle more ambitious projects, pushing creative boundaries in ways that might have been impossible otherwise. The inherent resourcefulness that is born from its use has had a trickle-down effect, fostering a culture of adaptability and problem-solving on set.

Moving beyond the technical aspects, gaffer tape's presence in a film or show can also tell a story about the production itself. A meticulously clean set, devoid of any visible gaffer tape, might suggest a highly controlled and professional environment, with a considerable budget dedicated to pre-production and set design.

Conversely, the visible presence of gaffer tape, while perhaps less aesthetically pleasing, can hint at the raw energy and ingenuity of a smaller-scale production, where quick fixes and resourceful improvisation were crucial to bringing the project to fruition.

The very act of seeing gaffer tape on screen can sometimes provide a subtle wink to the audience, an acknowledgment of the behind-the-scenes magic that made the scene possible. It's a quiet tribute to the craftsmanship, problem-solving, and resourcefulness that define the art of filmmaking and television production. It's a shared secret between the crew and the viewer, a silent nod to the countless hours of work and dedication that go into bringing a compelling visual narrative to life.

We can even extrapolate this further. Consider the evolution of special effects. The early days of cinematic effects were all about ingenious practical solutions, and gaffer tape was often a crucial component in those solutions. As technology evolved, the need for such ingenious fixes decreased, yet gaffer tape still remains a stalwart of production, a constant reminder of the resourcefulness and problem-solving skills inherent in the process. It is a legacy from a time of ingenuity and practical effects, a timeless reminder of how creativity can overcome limitations.

Looking back at the "tears in rain" scene in *Blade Runner*, the gaffer's swift action with the gaffer tape wasn't just about preventing a production setback. It's a microcosm of the entire process of filmmaking – a constant balancing act between planning, improvisation, and the ability to overcome unforeseen obstacles. The fact that this critical moment was resolved so smoothly, thanks to a simple roll of gaffer tape, speaks volumes about the often unsung heroes of the film industry, and the surprisingly significant role of the humble adhesive in bringing our cinematic stories to life. It's a silent testament to the enduring power of creativity and resourcefulness, held together, quite literally, by the sticky power of gaffer tape. And in the end, isn't that a rather beautiful and unexpectedly poignant metaphor for the entire film-making process? The magic, after all, is often held together by the seemingly insignificant—a powerful idea beautifully illustrated by a roll of matte black tape.

Case Study: A Sticky Situation

Our journey through the surprisingly cinematic life of gaffer tape continues. Leaving behind the rain-soaked streets of Los Angeles and the philosophical musings of Harrison Ford, we now find ourselves in a very different kind of sticky situation – the chaotic, yet often hilarious, world of reality television. Specifically, we're examining the production of a show known for its dramatic twists, unexpected alliances, and, yes, even the occasional strategic deployment of gaffer tape: *Survivor*.

While *Survivor* might not immediately spring to mind when considering the grand history of cinema, its reliance on location filming, often in remote and unpredictable environments, makes it a fascinating case study. The show's producers face a unique set of challenges. Unlike studio productions with controlled environments, *Survivor* relies on the unpredictable whims of nature – torrential downpours, scorching sun, and the occasional rogue insect infestation. This is where our trusty gaffer tape truly shines. It's not simply about securing cables and microphones; its uses are far more extensive and, dare we say, resourceful.

Consider the challenges of setting up challenges. Imagine constructing elaborate obstacle courses on a tropical beach, the elements constantly threatening to unravel weeks of careful planning. Wind, rain, and the ever-present threat of shifting sand make sturdy construction paramount. While heavy-duty lumber might seem the obvious solution, it's neither practical nor portable in the remote locations Survivor frequently uses. Gaffer tape, on the other hand, proves incredibly versatile. It becomes the invisible glue holding together makeshift structures, reinforcing unstable platforms, and securing essential equipment in the face of adverse conditions.

One can easily imagine the production crew, a motley collection of seasoned professionals and eager interns, grappling with a sudden squall, frantically applying gaffer tape to secure a vital piece of camera equipment perched precariously on a swaying palm tree. The drama unfolds not just on screen, but behind the scenes, a silent battle waged against the elements, with gaffer tape as the unsung hero. The narrative arc of this behind-the-scenes drama is compelling in its own right, a testament to the ingenuity and resourcefulness of the production team. They are pitted against the forces of nature, and their weapon of choice? A roll of black tape.

Furthermore, consider the myriad smaller, often unseen applications of gaffer tape. Repairing torn sails on a rickety raft during a challenge? Gaffer tape. Securing a loose microphone to a contestant's sweaty brow during a tribal council? Gaffer tape. Holding together a costume malfunctioning during a particularly intense immunity challenge? You guessed it – gaffer tape. It's the silent problem-solver, the ever-reliable quick fix, the ultimate backstage companion in the often-chaotic world of reality television production.

Beyond the immediate practical applications, gaffer tape subtly contributes to the show's aesthetic. Though hidden from the viewer's eye, its presence permeates the production, serving as a quiet testament to the behind-the-scenes efforts that go into creating the illusion of pristine, uncontained wilderness. The show's narrative is one of survival, resilience, and the unexpected twists and turns of human interaction. The unsung hero, quietly holding everything together, is the seemingly mundane roll of gaffer tape, a symbol of problem-solving prowess and unseen tenacity.

Now, let's move beyond the purely practical and explore the more metaphorical implications. In many ways, the *Survivor* production team mirrors the contestants themselves – resourceful, adaptable, and constantly facing unpredictable challenges. The contestants are struggling for survival, vying for the title of Sole Survivor; the production team, armed with their gaffer tape and problem-solving skills, are struggling for survival of a different kind – the survival of a successful production in an extremely hostile environment.

This parallel between the contestants and the production crew speaks volumes about the nature of reality television itself. It's a carefully crafted illusion, a meticulously constructed narrative built upon a foundation of improvisation, resourcefulness, and a healthy dose of luck. And at the heart of it all, holding it together like a well-placed bandage, is the humble roll of gaffer tape. It serves as a quiet reminder that even in the most extravagant productions, the simplest tools often prove the most effective.

This leads us to another aspect of *Survivor*'s gaffer tape usage: the element of secrecy. Unlike a movie set where visible gaffer tape might be considered a production flaw, Survivor 's use of tape is intentionally concealed. It's a behind-the-scenes battle against the elements, a constant struggle to maintain the illusion of untamed wilderness, a reality carefully managed and maintained by a dedicated team. The tape itself is an embodiment of this quiet efficiency; it's a solution that doesn't draw attention to itself, seamlessly blending into the backdrop.

The strategic application of gaffer tape in *Survivor* reveals a fascinating duality. It's a tool representing both the challenges and the solutions inherent in the production process. It reflects the struggle for survival, both for the contestants and the production team. In a way, it mirrors the show's central theme: the unpredictable nature of human interaction and the unexpected challenges life throws our way, and how we overcome them with ingenuity, resourcefulness, and sometimes, a roll of remarkably sticky tape.

Consider the sheer scale of the production: multiple cameras, extensive sound equipment, lighting rigs, and countless other pieces of equipment operating in often challenging terrains. The gaffer's skills are pushed to their limits – not just in the application of the tape itself, but in anticipating potential problems and proactively preventing them. This proactive approach to problem-solving mirrors the careful planning and meticulous preparation that go into creating each season of *Survivor*. It's a testament to the dedication of the production crew, their ability to think ahead, and their understanding that even the smallest detail can make a significant difference.

Furthermore, the sheer volume of gaffer tape required for a production like *Survivor* is a testament to its importance. Unlike a film production which might use tape for specific shots or effects, Survivor requires a constant and consistent supply, a reliable, adaptable adhesive capable of withstanding the elements and meeting the demands of a show filmed across many locations, weeks on end. This reliance showcases gaffer tape's value not just in its individual applications, but also in its overall contribution to the smooth running of the production, a constant, unassuming, yet indispensable companion.

Beyond the practical aspects, the use of gaffer tape on *Survivor* offers a unique insight into the intersection of artifice and reality. The show strives to depict a raw, unfiltered portrayal of human nature, yet its production relies on careful planning, meticulous detail, and a range of behind-the-scenes interventions, including the ever-present gaffer tape. This blend of carefully constructed illusion and genuine human interaction creates a fascinating narrative layer, a subtle tension between the manufactured and the authentic, a reality delicately balanced and held together, quite literally, by the adhesive power of gaffer tape.

In conclusion, *Survivor*'s relationship with gaffer tape is far from superficial. It's a case study in how a seemingly insignificant tool can play a crucial role in a large-scale production, showcasing the ingenuity and resourcefulness required to navigate the challenges of reality television filmmaking. It's a reminder that the magic of television, like the magic of film, is often found not in the grand gestures, but in the seemingly small, yet essential, details, the invisible glue holding it all together. And in the case of *Survivor*, that glue is undeniably, and undeniably effectively, gaffer tape.

Case Study: A Gaffer Tape Cameo

Let's move beyond the sun-drenched beaches and tribal councils of *Survivor* and delve into a completely different cinematic landscape: the meticulously crafted world of period dramas. Our case study this time involves the critically acclaimed series, *Downton Abbey*. Now, one might initially scoff at the idea of gaffer tape finding a place in the elegant halls of Downton Abbey. After all, this is a show steeped in tradition, where every detail, from the intricate embroidery on the ladies' gowns to the perfectly polished silver, speaks of a bygone era of refined taste and meticulous craftsmanship. But appearances can be deceiving.

The truth is, even in the seemingly seamless world of *Downton Abbey*, gaffer tape plays a crucial, albeit unseen, role (unlike the plastic water bottle that made it on set in a famously leaked photo). While it wouldn't be gracing the screen in any glamorous close-up, its presence is undeniably felt. Imagine the challenges faced by the production team: the sheer scale of the sets, the intricate costumes, the delicate props, and the need to maintain historical accuracy in every frame. Gaffer tape, with its versatility and relatively unobtrusive nature, becomes an indispensable tool in managing this complexity.

Consider the sheer number of cables and wires needed to power the lighting, sound equipment, and various other technical necessities hidden beneath the grandeur of *Downton Abbey*'s meticulously designed sets. These cables, crisscrossing the floors and walls, represent a potential hazard, not just for the actors but also for the delicate period furnishings. Gaffer tape, applied discreetly and strategically, keeps these cables safely secured, out of sight and out of harm's way. A stray wire tripping a meticulously placed antique vase? Unthinkable! Thus, the humble roll of gaffer tape becomes a silent guardian, ensuring that the elegant illusion remains intact.

Furthermore, let's not forget the complexities of costuming in a period drama. The elaborate gowns, intricate jackets, and tailored trousers worn by the cast often require adjustments on set. A quick nip here, a slight tuck there – all perfectly achievable, and invisibly achieved, with the trusty gaffer tape. Need to temporarily fasten a loose button or secure a trailing hem? Gaffer tape is the unsung hero, ensuring that the costumes remain pristine and historically accurate without interrupting the flow of filming.

Beyond the obvious practical applications, there's a fascinating argument to be made about the metaphorical significance of gaffer tape's presence in *Downton Abbey*. The show itself is, at its core, about holding things together. It's a story about a family navigating immense social and economic changes, about maintaining appearances in the face of upheaval, about sustaining relationships across generations and class divides. In a way, the unseen gaffer tape mirrors this underlying theme: it acts as the invisible adhesive holding the entire production together, just as the family and their intricate web of relationships hold together the fragile structure of their world. The show's seamless aesthetic is, in part, a testament to the invisible work done to maintain its integrity - a work in which gaffer tape is quietly but significantly involved.

Now, let's shift gears slightly and consider a completely different kind of production – the fast-paced, often chaotic world of live television. Let's examine a particular episode of *Saturday Night Live* (SNL). While SNL is known for its unpredictable and improvisational nature, the production team operates with a degree of meticulous planning and organization that often goes unnoticed by viewers. Behind the scenes, the frenetic energy of live television is tempered by a level of preparation and precision that demands flawless execution. Here, again, gaffer tape emerges as an essential tool.

Imagine the set changes during a live broadcast. The transitions between sketches are often incredibly rapid, requiring crew members to swiftly rearrange the stage, reposition props, and adjust lighting – all within the span of mere minutes. Gaffer tape acts as a quick-fix solution, temporarily securing props, securing set pieces, or subtly holding elements in place until the next segment. The pressure is immense. A single delay can throw off the entire carefully choreographed production. Gaffer tape allows for rapid adjustments and quick solutions to unforeseen problems, and it is frequently used to prevent potential mishaps. It's the silent partner in the hectic, high-stakes world of live television.

Consider, for instance, the challenges presented by the various intricate sets used in SNL. These sets are not simply static backdrops but rather dynamic elements that often require repositioning and readjustment between scenes. This involves the movement of heavy pieces of furniture, large backdrops, and potentially delicate props. Gaffer tape offers a reliable, quick, and relatively inconspicuous method for temporarily securing these elements, ensuring they remain in place during rapid set changes. It's often utilized to secure cables, wires and lighting rigs to the floor and walls without creating an aesthetically jarring presence. This allows the set designers to easily adapt to the unpredictable nature of live television.

Moreover, the unpredictable nature of SNL means that even the most meticulous planning can sometimes go awry. A sudden wardrobe malfunction, an unexpectedly dropped prop, or an unforeseen technical issue – these are all part and parcel of live television. Gaffer tape, with its immediate adhesive properties, provides a rapid solution to these issues, allowing the show to continue without interruption. Its flexibility and ease of use in improvisational situations make it a life-saver in the fast-paced world of live television production. A loose costume element, a quick repair to a malfunctioning prop, a cable needing temporary reinforcement – gaffer tape is the go-to solution, holding things together until a more permanent solution can be put in place.

Finally, let's think about the comedic potential that gaffer tape introduces, even in an unexpected environment like *Downton Abbey*. Picture this: a nervous crew member, frantically trying to secure a wobbly chandelier just moments before a crucial scene. The frantic application of gaffer tape becomes an almost slapstick moment, a silent running gag for those in the know. The invisible work of ensuring the smooth functioning of the production becomes a comedic subtext, adding a layer of humor to the behind-the-scenes chaos. In the high-stakes environment of live TV, where mistakes are amplified, gaffer tape acts as a silent problem-solver, often quietly rectifying issues so that the audience remains oblivious to the chaos behind the scenes. This unnoticed presence underlines the role of invisible infrastructure in supporting the smooth performance. It's a testament to the resourcefulness and ingenuity of the production crews and the power of an unsung hero – a simple roll of gaffer tape. The unseen glue that holds together the magic of the screen, regardless of genre, setting, or production style. The humble roll of gaffer tape provides not only a practical solution to numerous unforeseen problems but also offers a unique and often unnoticed narrative thread in many productions. Its versatility transcends boundaries and finds application in a variety of surprising settings, acting as a silent but indispensable partner in ensuring the seamless operation and visual integrity of countless productions. Its silent contribution to the cinematic and television world is, therefore, undeniably worthy of recognition and even celebration.

The Unexpected Star: Gaffer Tapes Unsung Role

The unseen hand of gaffer tape extends far beyond the meticulously crafted sets of period dramas. Its influence permeates virtually every genre, from the gritty realism of crime thrillers to the fantastical realms of science fiction. Consider the action sequences in a high-octane car chase, where the camera crew might need to rapidly secure equipment to vehicles or even to the vehicles themselves. The sheer speed and unpredictability of these scenes demand a quick, reliable solution, and gaffer tape often proves to be the hero of the moment. A strategically placed strip can prevent costly equipment damage, ensuring the smooth flow of the shoot without disrupting the adrenaline-fueled action unfolding before the cameras. The director's vision remains intact, thanks to the often unsung contribution of this humble adhesive.

Think about the complexities of a large-scale musical number, a whirlwind of movement, costumes, and lighting. Suddenly, a costume malfunction occurs mid-song. A rogue hem threatens to trip a dancer. A quick application of gaffer tape is all that stands between a flawless performance and a potential disaster. The show must go on, and gaffer tape silently ensures that it does, preventing a wardrobe malfunction from becoming a full-blown production catastrophe. It is in these high-pressure moments that its value truly shines through, a testament to its reliability and versatility.

The impact of gaffer tape extends beyond merely holding things together; it subtly impacts the overall aesthetic and look of a production. In the meticulously planned world of CGI-heavy films, where every pixel is carefully considered, gaffer tape's ability to blend seamlessly into the background (when applied correctly, of course!) is crucial. Imagine a scene requiring the use of chroma key, that famously green screen. The tiniest bit of unintended reflection or a visible piece of tape could ruin hours, even days, of painstaking work. In these circumstances, gaffer tape's ability to be discreet and yet highly effective is paramount. It's the invisible hand guiding the production process, contributing to the polished final product without drawing attention to itself.

Furthermore, the use of gaffer tape is not confined to the set itself. Its applications extend to the behind-the-scenes operations. It might be securing cables, preventing tripping hazards in dimly lit areas, or even acting as a quick fix for damaged equipment. The versatility is astonishing, transforming from a simple roll of adhesive to a vital tool for electricians, grips, sound technicians, and countless other production personnel. Its silent, unwavering support provides a reassuring presence in an often chaotic environment.

Consider the impact on post-production. The quiet dedication of editors, colorists, and VFX artists often goes unnoticed, yet their meticulous work forms the backbone of a film's visual impact. While not physically present on the set, the impact of gaffer tape may continue to influence their work. If lighting or camera equipment is held securely by gaffer tape during filming, post-production editors encounter smoother footage, devoid of the vibrations or irregularities that might arise from shaky camera work or poorly placed equipment. It truly is the silent, ubiquitous partner, facilitating seamless production from the pre-production stages through post-production refinement.

Beyond the technical aspects, gaffer tape plays a subtle but significant role in the storytelling itself. It's a tool that bridges the gap between the creative vision and the practical execution. Think about the use of gaffer tape in documentaries. It's unlikely to be seen on-screen, yet its presence underpins the ability to capture those candid moments. The ability to quickly secure cameras in unpredictable situations or to fasten microphones without drawing attention to the equipment allows filmmakers to capture genuine human experiences, enhancing the storytelling element. In other words, gaffer tape is the invisible narrative collaborator, contributing to the authenticity of a documentary's story by allowing for the effortless capture of authentic moments.

In horror films, where atmosphere and suspense are paramount, gaffer tape's unsung heroism is vital. The meticulous setup of each shot, the careful placement of props, and the creation of the unsettling ambience—all depend on the unseen support of gaffer tape. It might be used to secure elements of a set that add to the feeling of creepiness or decay, perhaps a loose floorboard or a flickering light. It's a tool that seamlessly integrates into the creation of atmosphere, adding to the overall effect without detracting from the narrative. It's a silent contributor to the genre's signature thrill.

The silent, effective nature of gaffer tape is often a reflection of the overall artistry of filmmaking. The best films often create a sense of seamlessness, effortlessly guiding the viewer through the narrative. The use of gaffer tape is analogous to this seamless storytelling – it's present in ensuring a smooth workflow, but its presence is rarely acknowledged unless something goes wrong. It operates behind the scenes, facilitating the execution of the director's vision without demanding attention to itself. This unassuming quality enhances the overall effect.

Even in comedic scenarios, gaffer tape can contribute to the overall comedic impact. It might be used as a prop itself, perhaps in a slapstick moment where something falls apart and gets hastily repaired with a roll of tape, creating a moment of unintentional humor. It's the subtle, unexpected detail that enhances the comedic effect. This unexpected appearance injects a touch of realism into the comedic world, highlighting the improvisation and problem-solving inherent in filmmaking.

The pervasive nature of gaffer tape is a testament to its adaptability and its simple, effective design. It is not burdened with complex mechanisms or intricate engineering; it relies on the simple principle of strong adhesion. This simplicity makes it an incredibly versatile tool, capable of handling a variety of challenges on any set. The very simplicity of gaffer tape underscores its brilliance—a testament to form following function perfectly. It does its job without fanfare, quietly ensuring the integrity of production across diverse scenarios. It is truly the ultimate underdog in the world of film and television production.

The narrative of gaffer tape is not just one of technical efficiency, but also of resilience and adaptability. It has quietly witnessed the evolution of filmmaking, from the early days of silent films to the high-tech productions of today. It has adapted to new technologies and challenges, always remaining a constant companion, a trusty ally in the often unpredictable world of film production. This longevity speaks volumes about its undeniable utility and its enduring place in the cinematic world. Its presence represents both the past and the future of filmmaking, highlighting the continuity of creative practices even as technology advances.

In conclusion, gaffer tape's role extends far beyond its basic function as an adhesive. It's a crucial component in the seamless operation of film and television productions, silently ensuring the integrity of the final product. From its inconspicuous support of complex CGI scenes to its unexpected appearances in slapstick comedy, it has quietly played a crucial role in shaping cinematic experiences for decades. It is, therefore, more than simply a roll of tape; it's a symbol of resourcefulness, ingenuity, and the unwavering dedication of those who work tirelessly behind the scenes to bring stories to life. Its story is a testament to the power of simplicity and the often-overlooked importance of the small details in the creation of cinematic magic. It is the unsung hero of the silver screen, a true star in its own right.

CHAPTER 3 - THE BANANA AND THE TAPE: A MODERN MASTERPIECE (OR NOT?)

Maurizio Cattelan's Controversial Artwork: A Closer Look

Maurizio Cattelan's *Comedian*, a seemingly simple artwork consisting of a banana taped to a wall using gaffer tape, ignited a firestorm of debate and controversy upon its unveiling. Far from being a mere piece of fruit haphazardly affixed to a gallery wall, the work became a lightning rod for discussions on the nature of art, the role of the artist, and the very definition of value in the contemporary art world. Its audacious simplicity, bordering on the absurd, challenged conventional notions of artistic merit and sparked conversations that continue to resonate today.

The piece's initial presentation at Art Basel Miami Beach in 2019 was nothing short of theatrical. Cattelan, known for his provocative and often darkly humorous works, presented the banana—a readily available, everyday object—as a high-concept artistic statement. The deliberate choice of a banana, a ubiquitous symbol of both nourishment and playful decadence, immediately underscored the inherent irony of the piece. Its placement, seemingly casual yet meticulously staged, further amplified the sense of calculated nonchalance. The use of gaffer tape, a tool commonly associated with behind-the-scenes practicality in film and theater, added another layer of unexpectedness to the presentation. Its humble functionality stood in stark contrast to the rarified atmosphere of the art world. The resulting juxtaposition—the mundane elevated to the status of high art—was both jarring and compelling.

The price tag of $120,000 further fueled the controversy. The exorbitant cost associated with a piece seemingly so easily replicated immediately questioned the very nature of artistic value. Was the value inherent in the object itself, the artist's concept, or the perceived exclusivity of the artwork? This question became a central theme in the ensuing critical discussions. Some critics praised Cattelan's clever subversion of the art market, highlighting the work's commentary on the absurdity of inflated prices in the contemporary art world. Others dismissed it as a cynical and opportunistic ploy to capitalize on the inherent fascination with the unconventional and the easily mocked.

The work's fleeting nature added to its mystique. The banana itself was perishable, destined to brown and decay. This inherent ephemerality directly challenged the traditional notions of permanence associated with fine art. The artist, aware of this inherent temporality, offered a certificate of authenticity alongside the work. This document confirmed the artwork's conceptual nature and its intended transience, further emphasizing the idea that the artwork itself was not the banana, but rather the concept it represented. The fact that the banana could be replaced did not detract from the work's value, according to Cattelan and his supporters. Instead, it highlighted the concept's supremacy over the physical object. This idea also directly challenged the very notion of unique artistic creation, an idea deeply rooted in the history of fine art and its valuation.

The media frenzy surrounding Comedian was unavoidable. News outlets, blogs, and social media platforms were flooded with images, opinions, and commentary. The debate transcended the usual confines of art criticism; it became a mainstream spectacle. The artwork's simple, almost ludicrous nature made it instantly accessible to a wide audience, regardless of their familiarity with contemporary art. This accessibility, however, also bred a diverse range of opinions, ranging from genuine fascination to outright ridicule. Some viewed it as a masterful commentary on the absurdity of the art market, while others condemned it as a frivolous and pointless gesture. The discussion touched upon issues of conceptual art, performance art, and the commodification of artistic ideas. It was a perfect storm of debate, fueled by the artwork's inherent simplicity and the outrageous price tag attached.

The controversy surrounding the artwork extended beyond its initial presentation. Several replicas, unauthorized yet undeniably similar, appeared online and in various other settings, further blurring the lines between original and copy. This underscored the inherent difficulty in defining the parameters of artistic ownership and authenticity in the digital age. The question of what constituted the "original" artwork became increasingly complex. Was it the original banana, the concept behind it, the certificate of authenticity, or the whole gestalt of the artwork as a media spectacle? All of these elements contributed to the artwork's complex identity, rendering the issue of authenticity more of a philosophical puzzle than a matter of simple verifiable fact.

The act of eating the banana, famously performed by artist David Datuna at the gallery, provided another fascinating layer to the ongoing conversation. This unexpected "performance," documented and shared widely on social media, further challenged notions of artistic ownership, the boundaries of artistic experience, and the very definition of what constitutes an artwork. It effectively highlighted the performative element of Cattelan's work, as the act of consuming the banana, though unintended by the artist, became part of its ongoing narrative. Did Datuna's act "destroy" the artwork? Or did it enhance it, transforming it into a participatory experience? These questions are still being debated by art critics and enthusiasts. The incident also raised ethical and legal questions regarding artistic vandalism, the boundaries of interactive art, and the potential liability of galleries in protecting artworks from such actions.

The *Comedian* saga, beyond its immediate impact, brought into sharp relief many critical issues within the contemporary art world. It challenged the established hierarchies of artistic value, prompting a broader discussion about what constitutes "good" art and who gets to decide. It forced a reconsideration of the relationship between the artist, the artwork, and the audience, highlighting the inherent ambiguity and inherent flexibility in that relationship. The discussion also prompted a re-evaluation of the roles of museums, galleries, and collectors in shaping the narrative and value of contemporary art. The controversy continues to resonate, prompting ongoing discussions about the complexities of the contemporary art world and the ever-evolving nature of artistic expression. In the end, whether you view *Comedian* as a masterpiece or a cynical stunt is largely a matter of personal interpretation. But its undeniable impact on the art world and the broader cultural conversation solidifies its place in art history, regardless of one's personal opinion. The banana, the tape, and the controversy they generated are intertwined, forming a unique and unforgettable moment in contemporary art. The piece itself is more than just a banana on a wall; it's a potent symbol of the complex and often contradictory nature of the art world itself. This, perhaps, is its greatest achievement. The lasting legacy of *Comedian* is not just the work itself, but the enduring conversation it sparked, a conversation that continues to evolve and redefine the boundaries of what we consider to be art.

Trenna Hoitytoit's Highbrow Perspective

The sheer audacity! The breathtaking... simplicity ! Maurizio Cattelan's *Comedian*, a banana secured to a wall with gaffer tape – a gesture so profoundly banal, so achingly minimalist, it transcends mere artistry and enters the realm of pure, unadulterated experience . One might even call it a zeitgeist. Or, perhaps more accurately, a zeitgeist-banana.

To simply label *Comedian* as "a banana taped to a wall" is to reduce it to the pedestrian, to the tragically unimaginative. It is, quite frankly, an insult to the very fabric of its being. We are not dealing here with mere fruit; we are confronting a potent symbol, a visceral representation of our post-postmodern condition. The banana itself, a phallic symbol of primordial fertility, is rendered inert, yet paradoxically empowered by its very immobility. It hangs suspended, a testament to the ephemeral nature of existence, a fleeting moment captured in a surprisingly sticky embrace of industrial adhesive.

Consider the tape itself, my dears. Is it simply gaffer tape? Or is it something more? Is it not a metaphor for the constraints of societal expectations, the adhesive bonds of conformity that bind us to a world devoid of genuine artistic expression? The very texture of the tape, its slightly rough surface, hints at a deeper, almost tactile experience of existential angst. One can almost feel the artist's struggle against the suffocating embrace of convention.

And the wall? Oh, the wall! It is not merely a backdrop, a passive observer to this daring act of artistic rebellion. The wall itself embodies the impenetrable barriers of the art establishment, the formidable edifice of elitism that dares to judge the merit of this… banana. Its stark, unyielding surface is a poignant reflection of the cold, indifferent gaze of the art world, perpetually poised to dismiss anything that dares to challenge its entrenched hierarchies.

The color, of course, is a critical component. Was it a particularly ripe banana? A subtly bruised one, hinting at the fragility of artistic genius? Or was it, perhaps, deliberately chosen for its slightly greenish hue, a subversive suggestion of the work's unresolved potential? I've commissioned spectral analysis on the peel's potassium levels. Preliminary findings suggest a complex interplay between the potassium's ionic resonance and the ambient gallery lighting, creating a subliminal aura of... well, let's just say existential dread.

The placement of the banana is not arbitrary, either. The precise angle at which it hangs—a matter of millimeters, I assure you—speaks volumes about the artist's subtle understanding of spatial dynamics and the psychological impact of asymmetry. Consider the implied trajectory: is the banana poised to fall? Or does it defy gravity, a defiant testament to the artist's unwavering will? The possibilities are endless, each one more profound than the last.

But let us not forget the audience, those privileged few who have witnessed *Comedian* in its full glory. Their response is, of course, crucial. The whispers of hushed reverence, the gasps of stunned admiration, the barely suppressed sighs of existential enlightenment – these are the true measures of the work's impact. Their collective reaction, analyzed and interpreted through the lens of advanced semiotics and psychoanalytic theory, reveals a deeply layered understanding of the artist's intentions.

Some critics, hopelessly mired in the mire of conventional aesthetics, have dismissed *Comedian* as a frivolous prank, a cynical attempt to exploit the gullibility of the art world. But such shallow assessments fail to grasp the subtle nuances, the layered complexity, the... banana-ness , if you will, of this extraordinary piece. These naysayers, blinded by their own artistic insecurities, are incapable of appreciating the profound implications of a banana carefully adhered to a wall. Their lack of insight is truly... bananas.

The price tag, an exorbitant sum in the eyes of the uninitiated, is not indicative of some crass commercialization. It is, rather, a reflection of the intangible value of the artistic concept. It is the price of enlightenment, the cost of transcending the mundane. Think of it as an investment in the future of artistic discourse.

The controversy surrounding *Comedian* merely serves to highlight its relevance, to underscore its provocative nature. The accusations of pretentiousness, of artistic nihilism – these are but testaments to the work's capacity to unsettle, to challenge, to provoke. It is a banana, yes, but it is our banana, a shared symbol of the absurdity of existence, a poignant reminder of the fleeting nature of fame, fortune, and perfectly ripe fruit.

Furthermore, let's not overlook the subtle humor. The juxtaposition of the commonplace banana against the rarified setting of a high-end gallery creates a subversive tension, a delicate balance between the mundane and the sublime, the trivial and the transcendent. This humor, however, is not merely slapstick; it's a sophisticated, darkly ironic commentary on the often ridiculous nature of the art world itself. It's a banana-peel on the polished floor of the art establishment, if you will. And who hasn't enjoyed a good banana-peel pratfall?

Finally, and perhaps most importantly, *Comedian* compels us to question our preconceived notions of art. What is art? Is it merely the skillful manipulation of materials, or is it something more profound, something that challenges our assumptions, that pushes the boundaries of our understanding? Cattelan's *Comedian* forces us to confront these fundamental questions, to grapple with the inherent ambiguity of artistic expression. And isn't that, in itself, the very essence of what makes art… well, art?

In conclusion, Maurizio Cattelan's *Comedian* is not just a banana taped to a wall. It is a multi-layered, deeply symbolic, conceptually rich, existentially poignant, and frankly quite delicious exploration of the human condition, the complexities of the art world, and the surprisingly powerful adhesive properties of gaffer tape. It is, in short, a masterpiece. A slightly overripe, but undeniably magnificent, masterpiece. And I, Trenna Hoitytoit, have the intellectual prowess to prove it. Now, if you'll excuse me, I have a banana to contemplate.

Trenna

JAMES ALLEN

Barry's White Van Wisdom: A Practical and Questionable Counterpoint

Right, so this fancy-pants art fella, Cattelan, sticks a banana to a wall with gaffer tape, and everyone loses their minds. A masterpiece, they call it. A zeitgeist-banana, even. Honestly, I've seen better stuck to walls. Like, that time I accidentally got a whole sausage roll wedged into the mastic on the inside of a customer's airing cupboard. Now that was a work of art. Took me half an hour to get it out, and the smell lingered for a week. But nobody's writing essays about that.

Look, I'm Barry, your friendly neighborhood white-van man. I deal in reality, not some abstract, overripe fruit-based conceptualism. My art is fixing leaky taps and navigating roundabouts at rush hour without incident. And let me tell you, gaffer tape plays a starring role in my masterpieces. But not in some pretentious gallery. It's in the everyday heroism of patching up a broken fence, securing a wonky satellite dish, or – my personal best – taping a rogue pigeon to a lamppost until the RSPCA arrived. That pigeon, incidentally, had excellent comedic timing; its squawks punctuated the entire operation.

This banana thing... it's got me thinking. First, the banana. It's a banana. You can buy a dozen for a fiver down at the market. It's going to bruise, rot, and attract fruit flies. Which, let's be honest, isn't exactly conducive to the longevity of a 'masterpiece'. You wouldn't hang a mackerel in a gallery, would you? Unless it was some sort of avant-garde statement about the fleeting nature of beauty, which I'd be more inclined to call 'fishy business'.

And the gaffer tape? Sure, gaffer's great. Versatile stuff. But this isn't exactly its finest hour. For a start, you've got the wrong kind of wall. If it's a plasterboard wall, which, let's be frank, most gallery walls are, you're looking at a maximum hold of about three hours before gravity – and probably a cheeky cough from a passing art critic – wins. Seriously, these city-slickers have no idea how to work with the stuff.

Now, if you're going for a truly lasting banana-to-wall installation – and I'm assuming longevity is a factor here, otherwise, what's the point? – you need to take a different approach. First, consider your surface. Brick? You'll need a seriously strong adhesive. Possibly a combo of gaffer tape and some good quality construction adhesive. Two layers of gaffer, overlapping, then a small blob of adhesive at key points. I'd probably use a type of adhesive that matches the mortar of the brick to ensure a good hold. We don't want that banana ending up on the floor or landing on some unfortunate art aficionado.

Concrete? That's tricky. Gaffer tape's not really designed for that sort of porous surface. You'd be better off using something designed for rougher materials. Like Gorilla tape. That stuff will stick to anything. A shark's teeth. A politician's promises. You name it. Still, use gaffer as a layer for easier removal.

On the other hand, if you've got a nice smooth painted wall, then gaffer tape might actually hold up for a decent amount of time. But even then, you're probably best using the heavy duty stuff. We're not talking about your everyday £1.99 special. We're talking about the good stuff: high-quality, professional grade gaffer tape. The type that has the strength of ten men but can be cleanly removed in a matter of minutes with absolutely no residue. Although, the removal of any adhesive really depends on the base of the wall surface.

And then there's the banana itself. Cattelan chose a banana. Why? Probably because it's cheap and readily available. But let's be honest, it's hardly aesthetically pleasing. The texture's all wrong. The color's… well, banana-y. Not exactly vibrant. It needs a little something extra, a touch of… je ne sais quoi.

I've got a few suggestions for banana alternatives. A perfectly ripe avocado? Now that's art. It's got a lovely rich green color, and a stunning texture. It's also considerably less likely to bruise and fall apart. You could even carve little designs into it! Alternatively, you can also use any other type of tropical fruit: Mangos, Pineapples, or even something more abstract, a grapefruit for example.

A bright red pepper? Visually striking. You could even use different coloured peppers to make a sort of abstract pepper-art installation. It would certainly look more vibrant than the banana. And speaking of vibrant, you can always use some neon-colored fruit, that would attract more attention to the artwork.

And let's talk about the ethical implications. Is it fair to just stick a banana to a wall and call it art? What about the banana's feelings? Has anyone considered its banana rights? I mean, the fruit goes through so much. It's a whole lifecycle – it has its struggles, it's born, it matures, and then it gets taped to a wall in a gallery. This should be considered as some sort of fruit abuse.

The art world's gone mad. They need someone to bring them back down to earth. Someone like me. A practical, down-to-earth, white-van man who understands the true value of good adhesive. And maybe a slightly less pretentious approach to art.

Now, if you'll excuse me, I've got a leaky pipe to fix. And I've got a feeling that gaffer tape might just be the solution. It's certainly less likely to attract fruit flies. But maybe I'll use the gorilla tape.

And before I forget, if you're thinking of replicating this masterpiece (or anti-masterpiece, depending on your perspective) at home, please take my advice to heart. Think about your wall, think about your adhesive, and think about the life cycle of that banana. Or better yet, skip the banana entirely and create your own masterpiece with something a bit more…durable. Like a sausage roll. Just remember, a good, strong adhesive is essential, and always clean your tools afterwards.

Thanks for listening!

B.

The Art of Controversy: Reactions and Interpretations

The internet, that swirling vortex of opinions and hot takes, exploded. Cattelan's banana, a seemingly simple act of artistic rebellion (or, depending on your viewpoint, a cynical publicity stunt), became the subject of intense debate. Art critics, their pens poised like sharpened lances, engaged in a flurry of pronouncements. Some lauded it as a profound commentary on consumerism, the fleeting nature of art, and the absurdity of the art market itself. They waxed lyrical about the banana's inherent symbolism, its connection to primal desires, its ironic juxtaposition against the sterile backdrop of the gallery. They discussed the ephemeral nature of the piece, the inevitable decay of the fruit, and how this decay itself was integral to the artwork's meaning. The price tag, naturally, became a major talking point; the audacity of assigning such a value to something so readily available and ultimately biodegradable fueled further controversy. Were they paying for the banana, the tape, the idea, the artist's reputation, or the sheer audacity of the whole enterprise? The question hung in the air, ripe with philosophical and economic implications.

Others, however, were less than impressed. The chorus of dissenting voices ranged from the politely skeptical to the outright scornful. "Overpriced fruit," sneered one particularly vocal commentator on a popular online forum dedicated to art world shenanigans. "I could do that with my lunch break!" Others pointed to the historical precedent of Dadaism and its embrace of absurdity, arguing that Cattelan's banana was merely a tired rehash of well-worn artistic tropes. The accusation of gimmickry was levelled frequently, highlighting the artist's history of provocative and often controversial works. Was this merely a calculated move to generate headlines, a cynical play for attention in an increasingly saturated art market? Or was there genuine artistic merit hidden beneath the peel? The debate raged on, fueled by social media and the relentless news cycle.

The arguments extended beyond the purely artistic realm. Philosophers weighed in, analyzing the piece through the lens of various schools of thought. Economists dissected the pricing mechanism, questioning the rationality of the market and the role of speculation in driving up the value of contemporary art. Sociologists explored the social and cultural context of the artwork, examining its relationship to celebrity culture, media hype, and the commodification of art. Even food critics got involved, offering their expert opinions on the banana's ripeness and potential culinary applications (though thankfully, no one dared suggest consuming the artwork itself).

The reaction from the general public was no less diverse. Many found the whole thing hilarious, sharing memes and jokes about the banana on social media. Others were genuinely perplexed, unable to grasp the artwork's supposed significance. Some were angered by the perceived elitism of the art world, highlighting the vast disparity between the price of the artwork and the everyday struggles faced by many. The banana, in its humble, slightly bruised glory, became a symbol of this divide – a point of contention that transcended the ivory towers of the art world and spilled into the broader public consciousness.

But beyond the memes, the articles, and the heated debates, a more intriguing question emerged: what exactly was the banana about? Was it a commentary on the art market's inherent absurdity? A statement on the fleeting nature of time and the inevitability of decay? A wry observation on our obsession with celebrity and hype? The beauty of Cattelan's work, and the reason it generated such passionate responses, lay in its ambiguity. There was no single, definitive interpretation. The banana, in its simple yet enigmatic presentation, invited viewers to engage with it on their own terms, to create their own meaning from its seemingly simplistic form.

This lack of a clear, easily digestible message contributed to both its success and its criticism. Some viewers felt cheated, expecting a profound revelation or a clear artistic statement. They saw only a banana and some tape, overpriced and undeserving of the attention it received. Others, however, embraced the ambiguity. They found pleasure in the open-ended nature of the artwork, in the freedom to interpret it according to their own experiences and perspectives. The banana became a Rorschach test of sorts, revealing as much about the viewer as it did about the artist.

Even the choice of the banana itself wasn't insignificant. The banana, a humble, everyday fruit, is readily accessible and easily understood. Yet, in Cattelan's hands, it became something more. It was transformed into a symbol, a potent representation of a multitude of ideas and emotions. Its seemingly mundane nature heightened the irony of its placement within the high-brow art world.

The controversy surrounding the banana and tape artwork extended beyond its immediate reception. Legal battles ensued over copyright and ownership, further fueling public interest and adding yet another layer to the complex tapestry of interpretations. The artwork's destruction, intentionally or accidentally (depending on which account you believe), only cemented its status as a legend, a fleeting moment in art history that continues to spark conversations and debates years later. Some argued that the destruction was a necessary part of the artwork's life cycle, echoing the banana's natural decay, while others lamented the loss of a provocative piece.

Perhaps the most interesting aspect of the entire affair wasn't the artwork itself, but the way it reflected our collective fascination with the absurd, our willingness to engage with provocative ideas, and our inherent need to assign meaning to even the most seemingly meaningless acts. Cattelan's banana became a microcosm of the art world, highlighting its contradictions, its eccentricities, and its capacity to generate both outrage and fascination in equal measure. It showed us that art doesn't have to be beautiful, or even comprehensible, to be powerful. Sometimes, a simple banana, thoughtfully (or perhaps not so thoughtfully) placed, can be enough to ignite a global conversation, challenge our preconceptions, and remind us that the definition of art is perpetually fluid and subjective.

In the end, the "controversy" itself became almost more significant than the artwork it surrounded. It sparked dialogue about the nature of art, its value, its accessibility, and its role in society. It forced us to confront our own biases and assumptions, to question the established hierarchies of the art world, and to reconsider our own personal definitions of what constitutes "art" in the first place. And that, perhaps, is the truest measure of a truly successful, albeit controversial, piece of art. It transcended the confines of the gallery walls and infiltrated the public consciousness, becoming a cultural touchstone for discussions about art, commerce, and the ever-evolving nature of artistic expression. It was a banana. But it was so much more than just a banana.

Beyond the Banana: The Power of Simple Materials in Art

The Cattelan banana, with its audacious simplicity, sparked a wider conversation. It wasn't just about a fruit taped to a wall; it was about the power of the commonplace, the transformative potential of the everyday. Suddenly, the humble banana, a ubiquitous symbol of tropical bounty and potassium-rich sustenance, had become a potent symbol of artistic provocation. And it wasn't alone. Contemporary art, in its often-unpredictable quest to challenge conventions, has embraced a startling array of mundane materials, transforming them into powerful statements about our world.

Think of the iconic works of Robert Rauschenberg, a master of assemblage who incorporated found objects – discarded newspapers, bits of metal, scraps of fabric – into his canvases, creating layered narratives that spoke to the detritus and dynamism of modern life. His "combine paintings" transcended the traditional boundaries of painting, blurring the lines between high art and the everyday detritus of urban existence. The inclusion of these seemingly insignificant objects wasn't gratuitous; it was a deliberate act of subversion, challenging the elitist notions of what constituted "fine art" and drawing attention to the overlooked beauty and potential inherent in the discarded. The humble newspaper clipping, suddenly imbued with artistic intention, became a potent symbol of forgotten news and ephemeral history. A rusty piece of metal, transformed by its juxtaposition with paint and other found elements, spoke volumes about the raw texture of urban decay and the inevitable passage of time.

Similarly, consider the works of Jasper Johns, who famously used everyday objects – flags, numbers, targets – as the basis of his paintings. His canvases, with their crisp lines and meticulous detail, weren't just representations of these everyday objects; they were meditations on perception, representation, and the very nature of art itself. The seemingly simple act of painting a number or a target transcended its literal representation, transforming into a deep exploration of the cognitive processes involved in recognition, the cultural associations we attach to these objects, and the subjective nature of our experience of reality. The stark simplicity of the images was a deliberate artistic choice, amplifying the impact of the mundane object and drawing attention to the layers of meaning embedded within our common perceptual framework.

The use of simple materials isn't limited to painting. Sculptors, too, have embraced the ordinary, elevating humble objects to new heights of artistic expression. Consider the minimalist sculptures of Donald Judd, constructed from simple geometric forms in industrial materials like plywood and steel. These works, far from being simplistic, were profound explorations of space, form, and the interaction between the object and the viewer. The deliberate lack of decoration, the clean lines, and the inherent simplicity of the materials themselves became potent elements in the overall artistic impact. The viewer was compelled to focus on the essential qualities of the object itself, its form and proportions, rather than being distracted by decorative embellishments or complex narratives.

This tendency towards simplicity extends beyond the realm of fine art. Consider the rise of street art, where artists utilize readily available materials – spray paint, stencils, even discarded packaging – to create powerful and often subversive statements in public spaces. Banksy, the anonymous street artist, epitomizes this approach, using readily accessible materials to create thought-provoking and often humorous commentary on societal issues, often challenging the very notion of "art" as something confined to galleries and museums. The ephemeral nature of many street art works, their inherent vulnerability to damage or removal, adds another layer of meaning, emphasizing the transitory nature of street life, and the temporary nature of protest.

The embrace of simple materials in contemporary art is not

simply a matter of practicality or economy. It's a deliberate artistic choice that carries significant weight and often serves a crucial purpose. It can be a gesture of rebellion against the perceived elitism of the art world, a challenge to conventional notions of artistic value, and a way to connect with a wider audience by utilizing familiar materials and objects. It allows artists to bypass the complexities of elaborate craftsmanship, allowing the core artistic concept to take center stage. In many instances, the simplicity of the material choices amplifies the power of the underlying message, allowing it to resonate more powerfully with the viewer.

The use of commonplace items also allows for a broader engagement with the world around us. The everyday objects used in these artworks often hold personal significance, evoking memories and emotions that the artist can share with their audience. A piece of old wood might conjure feelings of nostalgia, while a discarded plastic bottle might remind viewers of environmental concerns. This kind of emotional resonance transcends the formal aspects of art, fostering a more profound and empathetic relationship between the work and the observer.

In the case of the banana-and-tape artwork, it's not just about the simplicity of the materials but also about the concept it represents. The artwork, in its provocative simplicity, challenges established ideas about art's value and accessibility. The artist's deliberate choice of a readily consumable item like a banana underscores the transient nature of artistic creation, underscoring the artist's commentary on the fleeting nature of fame and fortune within the contemporary art world.

The debate surrounding the work highlights the subjectivity of art criticism. What one critic might dismiss as a mere gimmick, another might interpret as a profound statement on consumerism and the commodification of art itself. The reaction to such works reveals the biases and cultural contexts that shape our individual interpretations of art. The piece's ability to generate such intense discussion, irrespective of whether one considers it "good" or "bad" art, is a testament to its effectiveness in stimulating dialogue and challenging assumptions.

The "Beyond the Banana" discussion extends to other examples. Consider the use of found objects in sculpture. Instead of creating sculptures from meticulously crafted materials, artists might utilize materials scavenged from junkyards, construction sites, or even the streets. These materials – rusted metal, scraps of wood, discarded plastic – may not possess inherent beauty but are transformed by the artist's vision into compelling works of art. The texture of the aged metal, the grain of the weathered wood, the dull sheen of the plastic, all contribute to the overall artistic impact. The choice of found objects can add layers of meaning to the artwork, suggesting the themes of decay, regeneration, and the transient nature of material culture.

Furthermore, the use of simple, easily accessible materials can democratize the art-making process. Artists no longer need access to expensive studios and specialized materials; they can create art from materials found in their immediate surroundings. This accessibility can empower a wider range of individuals to express themselves creatively, fostering a sense of artistic inclusion and participation.

The broader implications of utilizing simple materials in art should not be overlooked. The use of everyday objects can spark creative thinking, encouraging us to look at the world around us with fresh eyes and to find beauty and meaning in the ordinary. It highlights the fact that art doesn't always have to be grand or elaborate; it can be found in the simplicity of a thoughtfully placed banana, a carefully arranged collection of found objects, or a poignant piece of street art.

In conclusion, the Cattelan banana, though seemingly simple, initiated a vital conversation about the use of everyday materials in contemporary art. This practice transcends mere practicality;

it becomes a powerful tool for social commentary, a challenge to conventions, a democratization of artistic expression, and a profound invitation to reconsider our perception of the mundane world around us. The banana, indeed, was much more than a banana. It was a catalyst, a conversation starter, and a symbol of the ever-evolving nature of art itself.

CHAPTER 4 - 101 WILDLY IMAGINATIVE (AND ABSURD) USES FOR GAFFER TAPE

Household Hacks: Everyday Solutions with Gaffer Tape

Let's face it, gaffer tape isn't just for Hollywood set designers and pretentious art installations anymore. Oh, sure, it holds a special place in the hearts (and on the hands) of those who wrangle wayward cables and precarious props. But its sticky, tenacious grip extends far beyond the glamorous world of filmmaking. In the humble realm of the household, gaffer tape emerges as a surprisingly versatile superhero, ready to tackle everyday challenges with its characteristic blend of strength and style.

Consider the perpetually perplexing problem of a wobbly chair leg. That agonizing squeak, the unsettling lean – the bane of many a dinner party. Forget those flimsy felt pads that wear out faster than a politician's promise. Gaffer tape, my friends, is your answer. A strategically placed wrap around the offending leg, adhering firmly to both wood and floor, provides immediate stability and a surprising silence. It's a quick fix that requires no tools, minimal effort, and offers a far more robust solution than those pathetic little felt things. And best of all, it's easily removable without leaving any sticky residue, unlike certain, shall we say, less refined adhesive tapes. (We're looking at you, duct tape – your reputation precedes you.)

But the chair leg is merely the opening act in gaffer tape's domestic drama. Imagine a picture frame, slightly askew, its precious contents threatening to slide into oblivion. No more frantic searches for tiny nails or precarious hanging mechanisms. A deft application of gaffer tape to the back of the frame, adhering it securely to the wall, achieves immediate rectitude. And unlike picture hooks, it leaves no unsightly holes – a boon for renters and neat freaks alike.

And what about that perpetually rogue cable, snaking across your living room floor like a particularly unruly python? Gaffer tape to the rescue! No more tripping hazards, no more unsightly spaghetti of wires. A few neat wraps, and your cables are tamed, neatly bundled, and ready to serve. It's a simple solution, but its effectiveness is undeniable. And the satisfying thwack of the tape adhering to the surface is surprisingly therapeutic. (I'm not suggesting you go around taping things just for the satisfying thwack , but if you do, I won't judge.)

The kitchen, that chaotic crucible of culinary creativity and accidental spills, also benefits from gaffer tape's unwavering support. A loose handle on a cabinet? Gaffer tape. A cracked tile threatening to unleash a cascade of ceramic chaos? Gaffer tape. A slightly frayed power cord on your beloved blender (the one that makes smoothies so convincingly like a spa day)? You guessed it – gaffer tape. It's the silent, efficient worker that keeps your kitchen running smoothly, even when you don't quite have the expertise (or energy) for more permanent fixes.

Now, let's venture into the bathroom, a space often characterized by its high humidity and its tendency to generate unexpected plumbing problems. A leaky faucet drip, drip, dripping away precious water and driving you to the brink of madness? Before you call a plumber (at exorbitant rates), try a temporary fix with gaffer tape. It won't solve the underlying problem (you'll still need to call a plumber eventually), but it can significantly reduce the drip, drip, dripping and buy you some time. Just be warned: you might find yourself developing a slightly obsessive relationship with the tape, regularly checking the faucet to ensure it remains securely sealed.

And let's not forget the children. (Oh, the children.) A broken toy? A ripped book? Gaffer tape can often provide a surprisingly effective – albeit temporary – repair. It might not be as aesthetically pleasing as a professional restoration, but it'll buy you some time before the inevitable meltdown caused by the irreplaceable loss of the beloved plastic unicorn. Plus, it teaches valuable lessons in resourcefulness, resilience, and the surprisingly satisfying properties of a well-placed piece of gaffer tape.

But the versatility of gaffer tape extends beyond mere repairs. Think about those unruly cords again, but this time, consider their aesthetic impact. Gaffer tape, in its various colors, can be used to create surprisingly stylish solutions. Instead of hiding those cables away, consider using brightly colored gaffer tape to create patterns and designs, transforming a chaotic mess into a surprisingly chic addition to your décor. (Don't tell your interior decorator I suggested this.)

Furthermore, the possibilities for creative crafting are virtually endless. Gaffer tape can be used to create unique textures and patterns in various art projects. It's surprisingly resilient and its strong adhesive properties make it ideal for creating both three-dimensional and two-dimensional artwork. Imagine the possibilities: intricate wall murals, innovative jewelry, or even whimsical sculptures. Its inherent strength allows for the creation of robust structures that wouldn't be possible with more delicate materials.

And who says that only professionals can use gaffer tape to make their lives easier? Let's face it: even a vicar needs a good, reliable, multi-purpose tape now and then. Imagine mending a tattered banner for the next church fête. Or securely attaching a precarious decoration to a delicate stained-glass window (a task better handled by gaffer tape than by Blu-Tack, let me assure you). This is where gaffer tape steps in to save the day – quiet, efficient, and entirely unobtrusive.

Even astronauts, floating in the weightlessness of space, might find a surprising use for gaffer tape. Sure, they have high-tech solutions for most of their needs, but what happens when a vital piece of equipment malfunctions and a quick fix is essential? A roll of gaffer tape, tucked away in a toolbox, could prove invaluable, offering a sturdy and reliable solution to a potentially catastrophic problem. And honestly, could you imagine a more dramatic setting for a triumphant gaffer-tape repair?

So, the next time you face a household challenge, don't reach for the superglue or the duct tape first. Consider the humble, yet mighty, roll of gaffer tape. Its versatility is astounding, its applications are boundless, and its ability to solve problems, both large and small, is truly remarkable. It's more than just a tape; it's a symbol of resourcefulness, resilience, and the surprisingly satisfying properties of a sticky, strong, and surprisingly adaptable solution. It's the ultimate household hack, and frankly, it deserves a place in every home toolbox

Creative Crafts: Gaffer Tape as an Art Medium

We've established gaffer tape's prowess in the home, its surprising cinematic cameos, and its controversial place in the art world. But now, let's delve into a realm where creativity reigns supreme: the world of creative crafts. Forget your precious paints and delicate pastels; gaffer tape, in its glorious, matte-finish glory, is ready to take center stage.

Think of it: a roll of strong, readily available adhesive, coming in a variety of colors, offering a unique textural element unlike any other crafting medium. Its very imperfections—the slight sheen, the possibility of minor wrinkles—add character, a certain je ne sais quoi that elevates the craft from mere hobby to avant-garde statement.

Let's start with the obvious: masking. While masking tape offers a clean, easily removable option, gaffer tape, with its superior adhesive, offers a firmer hold for more ambitious projects. Think intricate stencil work, where even the slightest shift can ruin the masterpiece. Gaffer tape ensures your design stays put, no matter the medium – be it spray paint, fabric dye, or even intricate airbrushing. The strong adhesion ensures crisp lines and a professional-looking finish, leaving traditional masking tape in the dust.

Beyond masking, gaffer tape becomes a medium in itself. Forget painstakingly cutting intricate shapes from paper; gaffer tape allows for quick, adaptable, and reusable shapes. Cut out geometric designs, floral patterns, or even free-form abstract shapes. Their vibrant colors provide a bold contrast against any surface, transforming ordinary objects into unique works of art. Imagine transforming a plain terracotta pot into a vibrant geometric masterpiece, the strong adhesive preventing any slippage or warping.

Consider its use in mixed media. Gaffer tape can be seamlessly incorporated into collage, adding texture and dimension. Layer strips of different colors to create abstract designs or use it to securely attach various materials, from fabric scraps to dried flowers, creating a textured, multi-layered artwork. The strong adhesive prevents elements from detaching, ensuring the integrity of your work.

The possibilities extend beyond flat surfaces. Sculptural applications are ripe for exploration. Using gaffer tape to create three-dimensional forms offers a unique challenge and reward. Begin by creating a wire frame, then layer gaffer tape to build form and texture. Experiment with varying colors and techniques – create smooth surfaces or deliberately textured, almost woven effects. The pliable nature of the tape lends itself to organic forms, allowing for unique and expressive creations.

Moving beyond purely visual arts, consider the unique tactile qualities of gaffer tape. Its subtle texture, almost rough yet yielding, invites exploration in tactile art. Create textured sculptures, or incorporate gaffer tape into clothing design. Imagine bold, geometric patterns adorning a garment, creating a piece that is both visually striking and texturally engaging. The tape's matte finish provides a sophisticated, subtly industrial feel that's both unexpected and striking.

Gaffer tape's resilience also offers unique opportunities. Its ability to withstand wear and tear makes it ideal for creating durable, long-lasting pieces. Consider creating textured jewelry or other wearable art; the tape's strength ensures that your creation can withstand daily use.

Furthermore, the versatility of gaffer tape extends to its ability to work with other materials. Experiment with combining gaffer tape with fabrics. Create stunning textile art, weaving tape into fabrics to create bold patterns. The tape's strength allows for intricate designs without fear of the structure falling apart. Imagine a tapestry woven with gaffer tape, creating a vibrant, modern take on a traditional craft. The contrast between the industrial tape and the soft fabric creates a beautiful tension.

For those with a penchant for upcycling, gaffer tape offers a unique method for transforming discarded items. Give new life to old furniture, using gaffer tape to create striking geometric patterns or bold abstract designs. The tape's versatility allows you to customize and personalize objects to create bespoke pieces. The surprisingly strong adhesive helps secure the tape to almost any surface.

Let's not forget the possibilities of light and shadow. The matte finish of gaffer tape, unlike many other tapes, doesn't reflect light intensely. This unique property makes it ideal for crafting light-based installations. Use different colored gaffer tapes to create a vibrant spectrum of light and shadow; explore contrasting textures by layering tape with translucent materials. The possibilities are truly endless.

Moving beyond the purely artistic, gaffer tape's surprising strength and adaptability make it a useful tool in other crafting techniques. Its strong adhesive can be used to temporarily bind materials together, allowing for intricate designs and complex constructions. It's a temporary adhesive, yes, but its strength in the meantime is undeniable. It's the perfect medium for creating temporary installations or sculptures that can be easily deconstructed and repurposed.

Imagine the possibilities: a temporary, vibrant installation for a gallery opening, showcasing the surprising versatility and inherent beauty of gaffer tape. The temporary nature of the artwork adds an extra layer of interest, transforming the experience into an ephemeral event. The artwork is gone but the memory—and the photos—remain.

Think of the potential for collaboration. Imagine workshops, where participants create collaborative art pieces using gaffer tape as the primary medium. The ease of use, the vibrant colors, and the surprising adaptability of the tape would encourage creative exploration and collaboration.

Finally, let's consider the environmental aspect. While not inherently an eco-friendly material, the reuse and repurposing potential of gaffer tape is remarkable. It's durable, reusable, and can transform discarded objects into unique works of art. By giving it a new life in craft projects, we can mitigate some of its environmental impact. The strong adhesive and durable nature of the tape ensures that the final product is as long lasting as possible.

So, there you have it. Gaffer tape, far from being a mere utility tool, emerges as a powerful and versatile medium in the hands of a creative individual. Its surprising strength, vibrant colors, and adaptability provide limitless possibilities. It's time to step away from the predictable and embrace the unexpected beauty of gaffer tape artistry. Get your rolls and start crafting! The world of gaffer tape art awaits! And remember, when in doubt, add more tape. The only limit is your imagination (and maybe your budget).

Outdoors and Adventures: Gaffer Tape for the Explorer

Now, let's trade in our crafting scissors for something a little more rugged: hiking boots. Because the versatility of gaffer tape doesn't stop at the doorstep; it extends to the great outdoors, where its adhesive prowess can transform a minor mishap into a triumphant expedition. Forget those flimsy, overpriced survival kits; a well-stocked roll of gaffer tape is your true wilderness companion.

Think of your trusty hiking boots, worn down after countless miles conquering trails and summits. A strategically placed strip of gaffer tape can reinforce those weakened seams, preventing a mid-hike disaster. No more limping back to base camp with blistered feet – gaffer tape offers a robust, reliable repair that can keep you going, even on the most challenging terrains. The secret? Its superior adhesive properties, gripping even damp or dusty surfaces, unlike other tapes that fail miserably when faced with a little bit of nature's grit. Forget those fancy, overpriced boot repair kits; a roll of gaffer tape is far more effective and significantly more affordable.

But its utility extends beyond simple repairs. Consider that unexpected downpour that transforms the trail into a muddy obstacle course. A quick application of gaffer tape to the soles of your boots will drastically improve traction, preventing those embarrassing (and potentially dangerous) slips and slides. It's a makeshift, yet surprisingly effective, solution that can make all the difference between a comfortable trek and a treacherous struggle. In fact, several experienced hikers swear by gaffer tape as a superior alternative to traditional mud grips, praising its longevity and reliability, even on the slickest surfaces. Don't just take my word for it; check out some online hiking forums. You'll find countless anecdotes of hikers using gaffer tape to conquer mud, snow, and even ice!

Let's move beyond footwear. Imagine you're deep in the wilderness, miles from civilization, and your trusty backpack strap snaps. Panic sets in, right? Not if you've got gaffer tape. A few wraps around the broken strap, and you're back in business, your precious cargo secure and safe. Its incredible tensile strength makes it ideal for this kind of emergency repair, providing a sturdy, reliable fix that can hold up under considerable weight. This isn't just for backpack straps either; gaffer tape is a lifesaver for broken tent poles, cracked water bottles (yes, really!), and even makeshift splints in the unfortunate event of a minor injury.

Speaking of injuries, gaffer tape's medical applications in the wild are surprisingly diverse. While it's not a substitute for proper medical attention, in a survival situation, its hypoallergenic properties and strong adhesive make it surprisingly useful for securing bandages, holding dressings in place, or even creating a makeshift sling. This isn't just conjecture; numerous survival guides actually recommend gaffer tape as a critical piece of emergency equipment. Its ability to adhere to skin (without being overly sticky or irritating) is a surprising but highly valuable asset in remote locations.

The versatility of gaffer tape in the outdoors isn't limited to repairs and medical emergencies. Think about those pesky insects that love to ruin a peaceful camping trip. Use gaffer tape to create simple traps to catch them before they can make your night miserable. Wrap it around a stick, coat it in something sweet, and watch the bugs become inadvertently sticky. It's a much more humane method than swatting, and far more effective than those useless citronella candles. Plus, you'll have a collection of slightly unfortunate insects to show off to your friends later (if you're into that sort of thing).

Then there's the matter of shelter. Need to secure a tarp for temporary shelter against a sudden storm? Gaffer tape is your best friend. Its strong adhesive ensures a secure grip, even on wet or windy surfaces. It can quickly transform a simple tarp into a surprisingly effective rain shelter, keeping you dry and safe while you wait out the storm. The flexibility of gaffer tape allows it to conform to any shape, providing a watertight seal even on uneven surfaces. It's the ultimate MacGyver solution for the outdoors, transforming a simple roll of tape into a vital survival tool.

Beyond practical uses, consider its surprising aesthetic value in the wild. Use brightly colored gaffer tape to mark your trail, ensuring you don't get lost. The vibrant colors are highly visible, even in dense forests or on snow-covered mountains. It's far more effective than the traditional, often easily-lost markers, and provides a sense of security knowing you can easily retrace your steps. This is particularly useful for hikers exploring unfamiliar terrain or during night hikes.

Even the seemingly mundane tasks become easier with gaffer tape. Need to secure a water filter to your water bottle? Gaffer tape provides a secure and reliable hold. Trying to hold your map in place while using your compass? Gaffer tape can do that. Want to attach your headlamp to a tree branch for better illumination? You know the answer.

The applications extend even further into unconventional survival situations. Imagine a broken fishing rod. Gaffer tape can provide a surprisingly strong repair, allowing you to continue your fishing efforts. A damaged tent pole? Gaffer tape can reinforce it. A ripped sleeping bag? Gaffer tape can patch it. The possibilities are only limited by your imagination and the length of your roll.

And let's not forget the less critical, yet still satisfying uses. Need to label your supplies clearly? Use gaffer tape. Want to create a makeshift bird feeder? Gaffer tape can help with that too. Want to leave messages for others on the trail? Brightly coloured gaffer tape is more effective than a scribbled note.

Let's delve into some specific scenarios where gaffer tape truly shines. Picture this: you're kayaking down a river, and a sudden gust of wind tears a hole in your kayak's hull. Panic? Not with gaffer tape. By carefully applying strips of tape over the hole, you can create a temporary seal, allowing you to paddle to safety. It might not be a permanent fix, but it's enough to get you out of trouble.

Or, imagine this: you're rock climbing, and a crucial piece of equipment breaks. A quick application of gaffer tape can temporarily repair the damage, buying you valuable time to get yourself to safety. It's not a perfect solution, but it's significantly better than nothing.

Finally, think about the sheer psychological benefit of having a roll of gaffer tape in your backpack. It's a symbol of preparedness, a silent reassurance that even in the most challenging situations, you're ready to face whatever comes your way. It's a small detail, but in the context of survival, that psychological boost can make a significant difference. It transforms a simple roll of tape into a powerful symbol of resourcefulness and resilience.

So, the next time you're packing for an outdoor adventure, don't forget your trusty roll of gaffer tape. It's more than just a tape; it's your emergency toolkit, your creative companion, and your steadfast ally in the wild. It's the silent hero of countless adventures, transforming a potentially disastrous situation into a triumphant tale of ingenuity and resilience. Remember, in the world of outdoor adventures, gaffer tape isn't just useful; it's essential. It's the unsung hero of the wilderness, quietly ensuring your safety and comfort in a way that few other tools can. So pack it, embrace it, and discover just how versatile – and life-saving – a humble roll of gaffer tape can truly be.

Automotive Adventures: Fixing and Decorating

From conquering the wilderness, let's shift gears – quite literally – to the world of automobiles. While gaffer tape might not replace a full engine overhaul (though, I've heard whispers…), its utility in the automotive realm is surprisingly extensive. Forget expensive auto parts and specialist tools; with a roll of gaffer tape, you're a MacGyver of the motoring world.

Let's start with the seemingly mundane: fixing minor damage. A cracked bumper? A loose trim piece flapping in the wind like a desperate flag? Gaffer tape is your swift and silent savior. Forget the costly trip to the body shop; apply a strategically placed strip of gaffer tape, and that unsightly damage becomes a temporary, yet surprisingly effective, solution. Remember, we're talking temporary here – unless you're aiming for a post-apocalyptic Mad Max vibe, in which case, go nuts! Embrace the rugged aesthetic. Embrace the chaos. Embrace the gaffer tape.

But gaffer tape's automotive adventures extend far beyond simple repairs. Think customization. Forget those overpriced aftermarket accessories that drain your bank account faster than a thirsty V8. With a roll of gaffer tape and a healthy dose of imagination, you can personalize your car to your heart's content. Want racing stripes? Gaffer tape. A custom hood decal? Gaffer tape. A subtle pinstripe along the side? You guessed it, gaffer tape. The possibilities are as limitless as your imagination (and the length of your roll).

Remember Barry, our white-van-man aficionado from earlier chapters? Well, Barry's got some "insider tips" on automotive gaffer tape artistry. "Right," Barry bellows, adjusting his stained overalls. "First thing's first, lads. You gotta get the right tape. The cheap stuff? Forget it. It'll peel off faster than a politician's promises. You need the good stuff. The sticky stuff. The stuff that'll hold a Sherman tank to a skateboard. Then, and this is key, you gotta prep the surface. A bit of a clean, a little bit of a rub, and you're golden. Then you apply it nice and neat. Like you're painting the Mona Lisa…only with tape. And if it doesn't stick? More tape. That's the motto, mate. More tape." Barry's advice, while lacking in technical precision, is nonetheless rich in pragmatic, if somewhat unorthodox, wisdom.

And the applications? They're as diverse as the cars themselves. Consider the humble headliner. Sagging? Unsightly? A strategically placed application of gaffer tape can give that drooping headliner a much-needed lift, transforming your interior from dilapidated to…well, less dilapidated. This isn't about perfection, folks, it's about functionality and a dash of resourceful ingenuity. Plus, think of the money saved! Consider that price tag on a new headliner compared to the pennies spent on gaffer tape. The maths speaks for itself.

Moving further, consider your car's exterior. Want to add some flair? Gaffer tape can be used to create custom designs, from simple stripes to intricate patterns. Think of it as temporary body art for your car; express yourself, experiment with different colors and designs, change it up whenever your mood dictates. It's a low-commitment, high-reward approach to vehicle personalization. And when you're tired of that particular design, simply peel it off and start again! This makes gaffer tape superior to permanent paint jobs, even if Barry would never admit it.

But beyond aesthetics, let's talk functionality. Ever had a loose wire under the dashboard, causing that maddening electrical glitch? Gaffer tape can securely fasten those rogue wires, preventing short circuits and saving you the expense (and frustration) of a potentially costly repair. Of course, it's crucial to ensure the wire is properly insulated first, but gaffer tape provides an extra layer of security, keeping everything neatly bundled and preventing any accidental contact. Remember, we're talking about temporary fixes, especially if we're talking about actual electrical issues – but they're effective temporary fixes nonetheless.

Ever had a broken sun visor? Gaffer tape's got your back (and your eyes from the glare). A few deft wraps, and your sun visor will be holding on tighter than a stubborn toddler to a candy bar. This is a surprisingly robust solution, allowing you to continue enjoying shade on those sunny drives.

Let's even step into the realm of car cleaning. Need to mask an area before repainting or applying a protective coating? Gaffer tape's precise application makes it ideal for creating clean lines and preventing accidental spills or overspray. While not a substitute for professional detailing, it can significantly improve the precision of your DIY projects.

Moving to the interior again, consider the versatility for securing loose items. A jiggling dashboard ornament? A rebellious floor mat? Gaffer tape can provide a quick and easy solution. While it might not be the sleekest fix, it's undeniably effective.

Even in the realm of automotive safety, gaffer tape can surprisingly play a minor but effective role. Imagine needing to temporarily secure a broken tail light cover while driving to a repair shop. Gaffer tape provides a crucial temporary fix, improving visibility and safety until the proper repair can be made. Again, this is a temporary solution for emergencies only. It's not a permanent substitute for proper functionality.

Beyond basic repairs and DIY enhancements, think about creative uses. Picture this: You're creating a custom car for a film or a themed event. Gaffer tape can play a significant role in achieving unique aesthetic effects, quickly applying and removing specialized designs, ensuring a quick turnaround for the project. It's the perfect material for temporary, bold statements.

However, a note of caution: Gaffer tape isn't a miracle worker. It's not designed for structural repairs or to fix major mechanical issues. If your engine's on fire, don't resort to gaffer tape. Call a tow truck. This is about creative solutions for minor inconveniences, not replacing vital car parts. The use of gaffer tape is meant to be temporary, providing quick fixes and creative solutions, not a permanent replacement for professional mechanics or expensive auto parts. Always prioritize safety, and remember that gaffer tape, while versatile, has its limitations.

To conclude this automotive adventure, remember this: gaffer tape isn't just a tool; it's a statement. It's a testament to resourcefulness, ingenuity, and a healthy dose of "get-it-done" attitude. It's the ultimate embodiment of "make do and mend" philosophy, applied to the world of cars. So, the next time you encounter a minor automotive mishap, before you reach for your wallet (or your phone to call a mechanic), reach for your trusty roll of gaffer tape. You might be surprised by just how far it can take you. Remember, temporary fixes don't have to look temporary with a little bit of creativity and a whole lot of gaffer tape. Now, if you'll excuse me, I have a loose hubcap and a rather ambitious design involving neon pink stripes to attend to.

Emergency Repairs: When Gaffer Tape Saves the Day

Let's face it, life throws curveballs. One minute you're serenely sipping chamomile tea, the next you're wrestling with a rogue garden gnome that's somehow managed to detach itself from its pedestal and is now dangling precariously from a power line. Or maybe, less dramatically, your prized possession, a porcelain frog wearing a monocle (don't judge), has tumbled from its shelf, shattering into a thousand pieces. Despair? Not if you have gaffer tape!

This isn't about meticulous restoration; this is about emergency repairs, battlefield patching, the kind of quick fixes that would make even MacGyver raise an impressed eyebrow (and maybe even borrow a roll for his next mission). We're talking about situations where the only thing standing between you and utter chaos is a roll of this wondrous adhesive.

Consider the humble bicycle tire. A puncture? A small tear? Forget the pump and the spare tube (unless you're a seasoned cyclist, carrying those is practically a badge of honor). A few deft wraps of gaffer tape, applied firmly and strategically, can often get you home, at least, avoiding a potentially embarrassing walk of shame. Of course, I'm not recommending this as a long-term solution – a permanent repair will eventually be needed – but in an emergency, it's a lifesaver, literally. Think of it as a temporary prosthetic for your bicycle's punctured pride.

Moving beyond two wheels, let's consider the four-wheeled variety. A flapping fender? A loose trim piece threatening to take flight at 70 mph? Gaffer tape to the rescue! While I wouldn't trust it to hold up against a major collision (I would suggest a visit to a proper mechanic in such circumstances!), for a temporary fix, it's remarkably effective. Remember that time I secured a nearly detached side mirror with it? It lasted long enough to get me to the auto shop, proving that it can be surprisingly robust, a temporary solution that manages to look…well, let's say "rustic."

The home improvement arena is where gaffer tape truly shines, in the realm of emergency repairs. A cracked windowpane? While replacing the entire window is ideal, for a temporary measure – preventing drafts, keeping out the elements – a clever application of gaffer tape across the crack can do wonders. Now, aesthetically, it might resemble a hastily applied Picasso masterpiece, but it's functional! And who's going to judge you when you're battling a hurricane-force wind, or trying to prevent a rogue squirrel from invading your kitchen?

Plumbing emergencies are, unfortunately, a part of life. A leaky pipe? Gaffer tape can create a makeshift seal, buying you time to call a professional. It's not a permanent fix, mind you. Think of it as a sturdy dam holding back a small river of water. However, this temporary solution stops the flood and prevents further damage until a more permanent solution is implemented. It's a testament to its versatility - from holding up mirrors to preventing a major plumbing incident, gaffer tape has you covered.

But gaffer tape's prowess isn't limited to merely utilitarian applications. Let's venture into the slightly more whimsical realms of emergency repairs. Ever had a particularly prized piece of art – let's say, a limited edition poster of your favorite band – suffer a tear? Before you descend into a despair-fueled meltdown, remember the gaffer tape. A careful application can mend that tear and bring back your artistic pride. Of course, it won't be invisible; it might even add to the artwork's character, introducing an element of "post-modern" repair aesthetics.

And what about those inevitable wardrobe malfunctions? A split seam on your favourite trousers mid-dinner party? A swiftly applied strip of gaffer tape can discreetly restore sartorial dignity until you can make a more permanent repair. It's a fashion statement that you never anticipated, yet it will prevent embarrassment.

Imagine: you're in the middle of a crucial presentation, your projector decides to rebel. The cable connector decides to give up the ghost. Panic sets in, the sweat starts, a disaster looms. But then...the gaffer tape. While it might not be the most elegant solution, a strategic piece of gaffer tape securely joins the disobedient cables, saving your presentation and preventing a career-threatening meltdown.

Beyond the mundane (or should we say, the mundane-ish), gaffer tape can be surprisingly useful in unpredictable circumstances. Ever needed to quickly secure a loose awning during a sudden summer downpour? Or maybe a flapping kite, threatening to escape into the wild yonder? Even repairing a broken toy for a crying child will quickly lead you to rely on the reliable gaffer tape.

The point is, gaffer tape is more than just a handy adhesive; it's a problem-solving superhero, a resourceful ally in moments of need. It's the unsung hero of countless emergency repairs, the silent guardian of countless mishaps. It's the epitome of quick fixes that hold strong and don't require complicated tools or excessive knowledge. It's the embodiment of that "make-do-and-mend" ethos, a philosophy that values ingenuity and quick-thinking above all else.

So next time you face an unexpected challenge, remember the versatile roll of gaffer tape lurking in your toolbox, your closet, your car, your camping gear. It's a testament to practicality, and it's ready to step up to the challenge – even if that challenge is a runaway garden gnome. Because life throws curveballs, but gaffer tape throws them right back. It's the ultimate emergency repair kit, packaged neatly in a roll, waiting for its moment to shine, saving the day, one sticky strip at a time. Now, if you'll excuse me, I hear a faint buzzing sound coming from my refrigerator... I think I may have a loose wire. Wish me luck! And maybe keep a roll handy.

You never know what emergencies await. The unpredictable nature of life always keeps us on our toes, and the humble gaffer tape provides the perfect quick solution. Let the repairs begin!

CHAPTER 5 - THE ENDURING LEGACY OF THE HUMBLE ROLL OF GAFFER TAPE

From Humble Beginnings to Global Phenomenon

The humble roll of gaffer tape. A seemingly insignificant item, easily overlooked amidst the chaos of a film set, the clutter of a workshop, or the curated chaos of a modern art installation. Yet, its enduring popularity and remarkable adaptability are testaments to its quiet power. This unassuming roll of pressure-sensitive adhesive has not only cemented its place in the world of filmmaking and stage production, but has also woven itself into the very fabric of popular culture, popping up in unexpected places and inspiring both practical ingenuity and artistic provocation. Its journey, from a relatively obscure industrial product to a globally recognized symbol of resourcefulness and creative problem-solving, is a fascinating case study in the unexpected success of a seemingly simple invention.

Consider its humble origins. While the precise date and inventor remain shrouded in the mists of time (a surprisingly fitting description for a product so often used to obscure things), its development is intrinsically linked to the evolution of other adhesive tapes. Duct tape, that stalwart companion of handymen (and women) and DIY enthusiasts, shares a familial relationship with gaffer tape, yet the two remain distinct entities, each with its own specialized strengths and applications. Duct tape, born from the need for a robust, all-purpose adhesive, boasts a more aggressive, less easily removable stick. Gaffer tape, in contrast, was specifically engineered for the demands of stage and film production. Its key characteristics – a strong but removable adhesive, a matte finish that minimizes light reflection, and a relatively strong cloth backing – quickly established it as an indispensable tool for lighting technicians, set designers, and countless others working behind the scenes of our favorite movies and television shows.

This specialized design isn't a mere accident of engineering; it's a direct response to the very real challenges of filmmaking and theatrical performance. Imagine the frustration of trying to secure cables and lighting fixtures with tape that leaves a sticky residue on the expensive sets and meticulously crafted costumes. Or picture the havoc of a brightly reflective tape ruining a carefully planned shot. Gaffer tape neatly solves these problems, offering a reliable and easily removable adhesive solution that's essential for the smooth operation of any production. This practical utility quickly led to its widespread adoption, transforming it from a niche industrial product into a ubiquitous staple in creative industries worldwide.

But gaffer tape's influence extends far beyond the confines of Hollywood studios and Broadway stages. Its remarkable versatility has led to its adoption in countless other applications. From amateur DIY projects to high-stakes engineering tasks, from emergency repairs to innovative artistic creations, gaffer tape consistently demonstrates its surprising adaptability. This adaptability isn't simply about its physical properties; it's also a reflection of human ingenuity. People consistently find new and inventive ways to use this humble roll of tape, pushing the boundaries of its potential and reinforcing its position as a truly versatile material.

Consider the seemingly endless array of uses documented throughout this book. We've explored its role in securing cables, mending costumes, temporarily fixing set pieces, and even creating impromptu props. But its applications extend far beyond the world of entertainment. The DIY enthusiast discovers its value in repairing leaky pipes, securing loose parts, and creating custom-designed solutions to unique challenges. The adventurer finds it indispensable for securing gear, repairing equipment, and making emergency repairs in remote locations. The artist, meanwhile, finds it to be a surprisingly versatile medium, capable of adding unique textures and visual elements to their work.

The story of gaffer tape is not simply a story of a product's success; it's a story of human ingenuity and adaptation. It's a reflection of our capacity to take something simple and transform it into something extraordinary, to find innovative solutions to everyday problems, and to embrace the unexpected possibilities inherent in even the most ordinary materials. Its enduring legacy isn't merely based on its adhesive properties, but on its ability to inspire creativity, solve problems, and quietly support countless projects, from the grandest cinematic productions to the humblest of DIY endeavors.

And then there's the cultural impact. The rise of gaffer tape as a recognizable item in popular culture is a testament to its versatility and pervasiveness. Its appearance in countless films and television shows, not just as a functional element but sometimes even as a visual prop or symbolic representation, has elevated it beyond its purely utilitarian role. It's become a subtle visual shorthand, a symbol of backstage activity, of problem-solving, of creative improvisation – even of a certain understated elegance. Its cameo appearances in films and television often go unnoticed by the casual viewer, yet to the keen observer, these moments serve as a silent nod to the behind-the-scenes magic that makes the magic on screen possible.

Beyond the world of entertainment, the recent surge in interest in DIY culture and upcycling has also elevated gaffer tape to a new level of cultural recognition. Its presence in online tutorials, crafting blogs, and maker spaces reflects its growing popularity as a versatile material for creating and repairing. Its image has also been integrated into various forms of artistic expression, further solidifying its place in the broader cultural landscape. The humble roll of tape, once a largely invisible helper, has become a subtly visible and recognizable part of our collective cultural consciousness.

Looking towards the future, it is certain that gaffer tape will continue to evolve. While the core functionality will likely remain unchanged – its strong but removable adhesive and durable cloth backing remain critical to its success – advancements in materials science could lead to innovations in its composition. The move towards more sustainable materials and manufacturing processes is also likely to have a significant impact on the future of gaffer tape. We might see the emergence of biodegradable or recycled alternatives that retain the key properties of the original while minimizing their environmental footprint. The demand for eco-friendly materials is growing, and it is reasonable to expect this trend to shape the future of gaffer tape production.

In conclusion, the story of gaffer tape is a surprisingly captivating tale. It's a testament to the power of simple innovation, a celebration of human ingenuity, and a reminder that even the humblest of materials can achieve remarkable things. Its enduring legacy is not merely a testament to its adhesive properties, but to its capacity to inspire creativity, to solve problems, and to become a quiet symbol of resourcefulness and adaptability in a rapidly changing world. It's a sticky situation, to be sure, but one that continues to inspire, innovate, and perhaps, most importantly, stick around. From the bustling sets of Hollywood to the quiet corners of home workshops, the humble roll of gaffer tape has earned its place as a true icon of the modern era, and its sticky embrace promises to hold firm for many years to come.

Conclusion - Gaffer Tapes Cultural Impact: Beyond the Practical

Beyond its practical applications in securing cables and holding props, gaffer tape's ubiquity has propelled it beyond the realm of mere utility, transforming it into a cultural icon, a symbol subtly woven into the tapestry of modern life. Its presence in popular culture is less about overt product placement and more about a quiet, persistent mirroring of the
resourcefulness and improvisational spirit it embodies. Consider, for instance, the countless behind-the-scenes documentaries and "making of" featurettes that showcase the frantic energy of film sets. More often than not, a roll of gaffer tape – a trusty, instantly recognizable ally – is visible amidst the controlled chaos. This visual shorthand instantly communicates a sense of practicality, ingenuity, and the often-frantic problem-solving inherent in the filmmaking process. It's a silent testament to the creativity and adaptability that define the industry.

The visual familiarity breeds a certain affection. Gaffer tape's matte black surface, its faintly sticky residue, its ability to seamlessly blend into the background while simultaneously holding things together – these attributes have inadvertently created a recognizable visual language, one understood even by those unfamiliar with its practical applications. Its appearance often triggers an immediate association with creativity, behind-the-scenes magic, and the transformative power of cinematic storytelling. It's not just a piece of tape; it's a silent participant in the creation of illusions, a silent witness to countless hours of hard work, and a symbol of problem-solving within a fast-paced, high-pressure environment.

This cultural infiltration extends beyond the world of film. Think of amateur theatrical productions, where gaffer tape, often repurposed and reused, serves as a versatile and economical solution to a myriad of challenges – securing set pieces, mending costumes, even patching up the occasional mishap. Its presence here reinforces its reputation for adaptability and cost-effectiveness, qualities valued not only in professional settings but also in grassroots creative endeavors. The humble roll of tape becomes a symbol of resourcefulness, a testament to making the most of limited resources, and a reminder that creativity thrives even within constraints.

The internet, a boundless repository of DIY tutorials, life hacks, and creative endeavors, further solidifies gaffer tape's cultural impact. Countless online videos demonstrate its versatility, showcasing its applications in everything from home repairs and crafting projects to quirky inventions and artistic expressions. This digital proliferation of gaffer tape's uses reinforces its accessibility and encourages further experimentation and exploration of its potential. The very act of searching for "gaffer tape uses" online reveals a universe of imaginative applications, demonstrating its enduring relevance and versatility beyond the professional domains.

The impact isn't just visual; it's also linguistic. Gaffer tape has entered the vernacular, becoming a shorthand for resourcefulness and quick fixes. The phrase "gaffer tape solution" evokes a sense of practical ingenuity and often carries a humorous connotation, suggesting a clever workaround to a problem. Its use in conversation is a testament to its cultural penetration, its ability to transcend its purely utilitarian function and become a part of the everyday language used to describe problem-solving, improvisation, and creative adaptability. This linguistic embedding reinforces its status as more than just a tool; it is a symbol, a metaphor, even a cultural touchstone.

Furthermore, consider the ironic juxtaposition of gaffer tape's humble origins with its appearance in high-art contexts. Maurizio Cattelan's "Comedian," a banana taped to a wall, is a prime example. While the artwork sparked a considerable amount of controversy and debate – some deeming it a cynical commentary on the art market, others finding genuine merit in its simplicity and provocative nature – it undeniably cemented gaffer tape's place in art history. The piece transcended the tape's practical functionality, becoming a symbol of conceptual art's ability to question the very nature of art itself and to utilize the most commonplace of objects to create profound and thought-provoking statements. The seemingly mundane gaffer tape was suddenly elevated to a central element of a high-profile art piece, blurring the lines between the commonplace and the extraordinary.

This elevation to high-art status further exemplifies gaffer tape's cultural impact. The very fact that it could be used to create a piece of art valued at such a high price – and that the piece's very existence relies on such a prosaic material – speaks volumes about the inherent versatility and unexpected potential of even the most ordinary objects. The piece's lasting impact lies not just in its monetary value, but in its ability to initiate conversations surrounding the nature of art, its accessibility, and its relationship to the everyday.

Moreover, gaffer tape's cultural impact extends beyond specific instances like Cattelan's banana artwork. Its versatility makes it a perfect stand-in for other, more specialized tapes in various DIY projects and home repairs. This substitution isn't just practical; it also speaks to the tape's reputation for reliability and strength. It signifies an implicit trust in its adhesive properties, a recognition of its ability to hold up under pressure, both literally and figuratively. This trust translates into a wider cultural acceptance and adoption of gaffer tape as a versatile and dependable solution to numerous problems, thereby solidifying its place in everyday life.

The enduring appeal of gaffer tape transcends its practical uses. Its cultural significance stems from its subtle yet persistent presence in our visual landscape, its integration into our language, its unexpected appearances in high art, and its widespread adoption in DIY and creative pursuits. Its story is a reminder that even the most humble of objects can, through sheer adaptability and unwavering utility, achieve an iconic status, becoming a symbol far larger than its simple form. It's a testament to the power of seemingly insignificant objects to leave an indelible mark on our collective consciousness, a testament to the enduring power of a simple, sticky roll of tape. And in a world constantly seeking innovative solutions, this humble tape continues to stick with us, holding things together, both literally and metaphorically. The stickiness, it seems, is here to stay.

The Future of Gaffer Tape: Innovation and Sustainability

The enduring success of gaffer tape hinges not only on its present utility but also on its potential for future innovation. While the basic principle – a strong, versatile adhesive on a cloth backing – remains constant, the materials and manufacturing processes are ripe for disruption. Imagine a gaffer tape crafted from entirely recycled materials, its adhesive derived from sustainably sourced plant-based polymers instead of petroleum products. Such a development wouldn't just reduce the environmental impact of this ubiquitous product; it would also resonate deeply with consumers increasingly concerned about sustainability. The shift towards eco-conscious manufacturing is not merely a trend; it's a necessity, and gaffer tape, like countless other products, will need to adapt to survive.

This transition, however, wouldn't necessarily compromise performance. In fact, innovation could lead to a superior product. Imagine a bio-based adhesive that's even stickier, more resistant to temperature fluctuations, or even biodegradable after its useful life. The possibilities are vast. Research into new adhesives is ongoing, with scientists exploring everything from microbial sources to modified starches and cellulose derivatives. The potential for advancements in the backing material is equally exciting. Imagine a stronger, lighter, yet more flexible fabric, perhaps incorporating nanotechnology for improved durability and resilience. Such innovations could result in a gaffer tape that is not only environmentally friendly but also surpasses the performance of its petroleum-based predecessors.

Beyond material science, the future of gaffer tape may also involve smart technology. Imagine a tape embedded with sensors that monitor its adhesion strength, alerting users when it's nearing the end of its life or if its bond is compromised. This would reduce waste and prevent accidents, particularly in critical applications like stage lighting or film production. Furthermore, the integration of smart technology could facilitate better inventory management and supply chain optimization, leading to reduced costs and improved efficiency for manufacturers and consumers alike. We could see smart packaging that alerts users to remaining length, ensuring less waste and optimizing usage. The potential for data collection could also inform further research into material science and adhesive performance, creating a feedback loop that drives ongoing improvement.

The integration of smart technology might even extend beyond simple sensors. Imagine a gaffer tape that changes color to indicate its adherence strength, or one that glows in the dark to improve visibility in low-light conditions. These might seem like fanciful notions, but considering the rapid pace of technological advancement, they're not as far-fetched as they may appear. The possibilities for customization are endless. Specialized gaffer tapes could be developed for specific applications, with varying levels of adhesion, color, and even texture optimized for particular needs. We could see gaffer tapes designed specifically for underwater use, for high-temperature environments, or for applications requiring exceptionally high tensile strength.

The convergence of sustainability and technology is poised to redefine the future of gaffer tape. Companies are already experimenting with recycled materials and exploring new, eco-friendly manufacturing processes. This trend is driven not only by environmental concerns but also by the growing demand for ethical and sustainable consumer products. Consumers are becoming increasingly aware of the environmental footprint of their purchases, and companies that fail to adapt to this changing landscape will be left behind. The future of gaffer tape is not just about sticking things together; it's about aligning with the values of a more environmentally responsible world.

However, the challenge isn't just about innovation; it's about accessibility. Sustainable materials and advanced technologies often come with a higher initial cost. To ensure that the benefits of these advancements reach a wider audience, efforts need to be made to reduce the price point of eco-friendly gaffer tape. This might involve government subsidies, incentives for sustainable manufacturing, or economies of scale as production ramps up. It's crucial to ensure that sustainable alternatives aren't relegated to a niche market but become the standard, accessible to everyone, from professional film crews to DIY enthusiasts.

Another aspect to consider is the potential for new, disruptive technologies to challenge the dominance of gaffer tape altogether.

While its versatility and reliability have ensured its continued success, other adhesive technologies may emerge that offer superior performance or cost-effectiveness. These might involve advanced adhesives with unique properties, or entirely new methods of securing objects without tape. However, it's unlikely that any single technology will entirely replace gaffer tape. Its versatility and ease of use have cemented its place in numerous industries, and its cultural significance ensures its continued presence. But future success will depend on its ability to adapt and innovate, incorporating sustainable practices and embracing technological advancements.

The future of gaffer tape isn't just about sticking to the past; it's about cleverly sticking to the future. The inherent adaptability that made gaffer tape a staple in the first place is precisely what will guide its evolution. The challenge is to maintain its tried-and-true functionality while seamlessly integrating sustainable practices and innovative technologies. This balancing act will ensure that the humble roll of tape remains not only a vital tool but also a symbol of resourceful ingenuity for generations to come. The sticky situation, in other words, is far from over. The future of gaffer tape is as bright and potentially sticky as ever, a testament to its surprisingly enduring legacy. Its evolution is a microcosm of the larger shift towards a more sustainable and technologically advanced future, reminding us that even the most unassuming objects can play a significant role in the larger narrative of progress. The quiet, unassuming roll of tape may well have a very loud future ahead.

The impact of sustainability extends beyond the materials themselves. The entire supply chain needs consideration. Where will the raw materials come from? How will the manufacturing process minimize its carbon footprint? What strategies will be used to minimize waste and promote recycling at the end of the tape's life cycle? These are complex questions that require collaboration between manufacturers, researchers, and policymakers. Life cycle assessments—a detailed examination of a product's environmental impact from cradle to grave—are crucial in determining the true sustainability of any new gaffer tape alternative. Transparency in reporting these assessments will build consumer trust and drive the market towards genuinely environmentally friendly options.

Moreover, the future of gaffer tape involves thinking beyond its traditional applications. As the world shifts towards more sustainable practices, opportunities will emerge for its use in environmentally conscious initiatives. Imagine a gaffer tape used in repairing damaged ecosystems, for instance, helping to secure protective barriers or hold together delicate plant life during restoration projects. The adaptability that has made it a staple in filmmaking and DIY projects could translate to surprising new applications in fields like environmental science, conservation, and even disaster relief.

The inherent stickiness of gaffer tape, both literally and metaphorically, represents a tenacious quality that will ensure its future. It's a symbol of resilience, adaptability, and resourceful ingenuity. While technological advancements may reshape its composition and manufacturing, the core values of practicality, versatility, and ease of use are likely to remain its defining features. The journey towards a more sustainable and technologically advanced gaffer tape is a testament to human ingenuity and our commitment to finding innovative solutions to even the smallest of challenges. This humble roll of tape, with its remarkable history, has a future as sticky and exciting as its past. And that, my friends, is something worth sticking with.

Celebrating the Versatility: A Final Word

But let's not dwell on the future just yet. Let's celebrate the present – the sheer, unadulterated versatility of gaffer tape. We've journeyed from its humble beginnings, tracing its evolution and its unexpected stardom in the world of cinema and art. We've even grappled with the philosophical implications of a banana strategically adhered to a wall. Now, it's time to truly appreciate the breadth of this sticky wonder's capabilities.

Think about it: gaffer tape isn't just for holding things together; it's a problem-solving maestro, a quick-fix artist, a silent, sticky superhero. It's the MacGyver of the adhesive world, capable of tackling challenges that would stump even the most seasoned engineer (though perhaps not Barry, the White-Van Man, who'd likely approach any scenario with a charming disregard for conventional wisdom and a healthy dose of superglue).

Its uses are as diverse as the people who employ it. Consider the humble vicar, for instance, using it to discreetly mend a rip in his surplice during a particularly boisterous Christmas carol service. Or the intrepid astronaut, employing it to secure a vital piece of equipment during a spacewalk – a minor repair with potentially enormous consequences. Picture a frantic plumber, patching a burst pipe with a piece of gaffer tape and a prayer (though, ideally, he'd also have a proper pipe wrench handy). Even the enigmatic mime artist finds it invaluable, using it to create temporary props or to subtly enhance the visual impact of their silent performance.

The versatility extends beyond the practical. Think of the artist, using gaffer tape not as a means of repair, but as a medium in itself. Its texture, its subtle sheen, its ability to hold and yet remain relatively unobtrusive: these qualities have inspired creativity in ways that even its inventors might never have imagined. Indeed, the very concept of using gaffer tape as a primary artistic element challenges conventional notions of art, blurring the line between functionality and aesthetics.

Beyond the artistic realm, consider the sheer variety of everyday situations where gaffer tape proves itself invaluable. A quick fix for a loose wire, a temporary repair for a broken toy, a secure hold for posters on a wall (or, if you're Barry, for just about anything on any wall). It's the ultimate household hero, quietly tackling problems with a silent efficiency that belies its simplicity.

We haven't even begun to scratch the surface of its potential. Think of the possibilities in the realm of fashion. Imagine designers incorporating gaffer tape into avant-garde garments – textured elements, structural supports, even unique embellishments. It could easily become a high-fashion statement, a bold juxtaposition of rugged functionality and high-end aesthetics.

The automotive world, too, offers possibilities. While not a replacement for proper repairs, gaffer tape's temporary sticking power could be invaluable for quick fixes on the road. Of course, we wouldn't recommend relying on it for major engine repairs, but for a temporary fix to a loose panel or a flapping fender, it's a surprisingly resourceful tool.

Then there's the culinary potential, albeit a more niche application. While we wouldn't recommend using it to seal your casserole (unless you're particularly adventurous and willing to sacrifice a good oven cleaner), its inherent stickiness could have creative uses in the world of avant-garde desserts, perhaps as a structural element in a complex confectionery masterpiece.

Of course, we must acknowledge the limitations. Gaffer tape isn't a cure-all. It won't fix a broken heart, mend a fractured friendship, or solve the climate crisis (though, as we've discussed, a move toward sustainable manufacturing would be a step in the right direction). It's not meant for long-term solutions in scenarios requiring serious structural integrity. Trying to use it to hold up a collapsing building would be, let's just say, unwise.

But within its practical limitations, its versatility is truly remarkable. It's a testament to the power of simple, well-designed materials, a reminder that ingenious solutions often come from unexpectedly humble sources. This seemingly unassuming roll of tape embodies the spirit of resourcefulness, a practical magic that's always within reach. It is, in its own quiet way, a symbol of human creativity, adapting and finding solutions for an endless number of situations.

This isn't just about the physical properties of gaffer tape; it's about the mindset it inspires. It's a reminder that there's often a creative, resourceful solution to be found, even in seemingly impossible situations. It's a call to embrace ingenuity, to think outside the box, and to find the unexpected joy in problem-solving.

So, let's raise a metaphorical toast (perhaps with a stick of exceptionally strong chewing gum held together with... you guessed it... gaffer tape) to the humble roll of tape. To its enduring legacy, its surprisingly captivating history, and its truly unparalleled versatility. It's a small thing, perhaps, but its impact is undeniably large. It's a staple in workshops and studios, a silent partner in countless adventures, a testament to human ingenuity and resourcefulness. And that, my friends, is a legacy worth celebrating. So go forth and stick things together. The world, in all its chaotic glory, needs all the sticky solutions it can get.

And if you happen to find yourself needing to create a modern art masterpiece featuring a banana, remember: there's always gaffer tape. And perhaps a little bit of Barry's surprisingly effective (if slightly questionable) advice on wall adhesion. After all, who knows? Your next masterpiece might just be waiting to be stuck in place.

This humble roll of tape, easily overlooked, has quietly woven its way into the fabric of our lives, proving that sometimes, the most remarkable things are also the most unassuming. From the glamorous sets of Hollywood blockbusters to the humble DIY projects in our homes, gaffer tape's presence is a constant reminder of the power of simple solutions, of resourcefulness, and of the surprising creativity that can be unleashed when we embrace the humble and unexpected. And that's a legacy worth sticking with, indeed. We haven't exhausted all the possibilities, not by a long shot. The ongoing creativity surrounding gaffer tape, both practical and artistic, ensures its enduring place in our lives, a testament to its versatile nature and our boundless human ingenuity.

Let's revisit the vicar, the astronaut, and the plumber once more. Each represents a different facet of gaffer tape's versatility. The vicar's use highlights its ability to discreetly solve a problem, a quiet efficiency that goes unnoticed but provides vital support. The astronaut's reliance on gaffer tape underscores its reliability in extreme conditions, its ability to perform under pressure and contribute to a larger, more significant mission. Finally, the plumber's use of gaffer tape showcases its immediate practicality, a quick fix that prevents greater damage and inconvenience. These diverse examples paint a vivid picture of the scope of gaffer tape's usefulness, highlighting its adaptability across various sectors and contexts.

Consider, too, the less glamorous but equally crucial roles of gaffer tape. It's the unsung hero of countless industrial applications, the silent worker holding together machinery, securing cables, and ensuring the smooth operation of various processes. It's the backbone of many everyday functions that we take for granted but are vital to our way of life. In this aspect, it's a symbol of unseen labor, a reminder that even the most ordinary materials play a crucial part in the larger scheme of things.

So, the next time you reach for a roll of gaffer tape, take a moment to appreciate its versatility, its resilience, and its surprisingly captivating history. It's more than just a roll of tape; it's a symbol of resourcefulness, creativity, and the enduring power of simple solutions. It's a reminder that the most remarkable things are often found in the most unexpected places, quietly and efficiently doing their jobs, holding things together, one sticky strip at a time. And that, quite simply, is something truly remarkable. It's a testament to the enduring legacy of a humble roll of tape—a legacy that is, quite literally, stuck with us for the long haul.

A Sticky Farewell: Further Exploration

The sheer, tenacious grip of gaffer tape on our collective consciousness begs the question: where do we go from here? Having explored its cinematic cameos, its artistic pretensions (thanks, Maurizio!), and its surprisingly diverse practical applications, we find ourselves at a sticky juncture, poised to consider the future of this unsung hero of the adhesive world. But before we leap into speculative realms of self-healing tape and bio-degradable sticky solutions, let's linger a little longer in the present, savoring the simple, yet profound, reality of the humble roll.

One might argue that the true legacy of gaffer tape isn't in its future innovations, but in its enduring ability to inspire. Its quiet functionality is a testament to the power of problem-solving, a reminder that ingenious solutions often arrive not in a flash of brilliance, but in the readily available tools at hand. Think of the countless impromptu repairs, the countless quick fixes, the countless times gaffer tape has saved the day (or at least, saved a presentation). Its legacy is woven into the fabric of everyday life, a silent, sticky thread connecting countless moments of resourcefulness and ingenuity.

This brings us to the realm of creative exploration. The versatility of gaffer tape transcends mere utility; it's a canvas for the imagination. Consider the possibilities: gaffer tape sculptures, gaffer tape mosaics, even gaffer tape fashion (we're not judging!). The limitations are only as constricting as your imagination. Let your creativity run wild. Think beyond repairs and into the realm of artistic expression. Imagine a world where gaffer tape isn't just a tool, but a medium.

This is where the "sticky farewell" truly comes into play. We're not saying goodbye to gaffer tape; rather, we're urging you to embrace its potential, to explore its capabilities beyond what you might initially consider. The journey of discovery doesn't end with this book; in fact, it's just beginning. We've laid the groundwork, provided the inspiration, and now it's your turn to take the reins.

So, how do we continue this exploration? The possibilities are as numerous as the applications of gaffer tape itself. Here are a few suggestions to help you delve deeper into the wonderfully sticky world of this versatile adhesive:

1. The Great Gaffer Tape Challenge: Gather your friends, family, or colleagues and embark on a creative challenge. Set a time limit and see who can come up with the most innovative and practical uses for gaffer tape. The winner, of course, gets bragging rights and maybe a lifetime supply (or, at least, a very large roll) of their favorite adhesive. Think outside the box! This challenge can be adapted to suit any age group or skill level. Children might create whimsical tape creatures, while adults might tackle more complex problem-solving scenarios. The possibilities are endless.

2. Gaffer Tape Art Project: Take inspiration from Maurizio Cattelan's banana masterpiece (or, let's be honest, the myriad of banana-tape tributes that followed). Create your own gaffer tape art. Experiment with different colors, textures, and shapes. Don't be afraid to embrace the absurdity – remember, the inherent silliness of the medium can be its greatest strength. Document your creations and share them online, inspiring others to join

the sticky revolution. Perhaps a hashtag like GafferTapeArt could build a vibrant online community.

3. The Gaffer Tape Field Guide: Compile a comprehensive field guide to gaffer tape, documenting its various applications, its strengths and weaknesses in different contexts, and its historical significance. This could be a personal project, a class assignment, or even a collaborative effort. The field guide could include detailed instructions, color photos, and insightful commentary on the nuances of this ubiquitous tape. It could cover everything from basic repairs to advanced techniques, making it a valuable resource for anyone who wants to master the art of gaffer tape.

4. Gaffer Tape Time Capsule: Assemble a time capsule featuring objects secured with gaffer tape. This project allows for reflection on the present while anticipating the future. Include items that represent your current passions, hobbies, or ambitions. Seal the capsule with, naturally, copious amounts of gaffer tape, and set a date for its opening – perhaps ten years, twenty years, or even longer. This will provide a unique and entertaining glimpse into the past. Consider including a note explaining the significance of gaffer tape in your life and its enduring legacy.

5. Gaffer Tape Documentary: Create a short documentary exploring the history, uses, and cultural impact of gaffer tape. Interview people from different walks of life to showcase the tape's versatility and its role in various industries. From electricians to artists, plumbers to filmmakers, each individual's experience would contribute to a fascinating mosaic of gaffer tape's influence on our world. The documentary could feature captivating visuals, showcasing the tape in action, highlighting its unique properties, and exploring its significance in human history.

6. A Gaffer Tape-Themed Party: Organize a party centered around the humble roll of tape. Guests could participate in gaffer tape-related activities, such as a blindfolded tape-wrapping challenge

or a gaffer tape sculpture competition. The decorations could feature an abundance of colorful tape, and the party favors could be small rolls of gaffer tape personalized with guests' names. The entire affair would be a lighthearted and fun celebration of this versatile material and its surprising influence on modern culture.

These suggestions, of course, only scratch the surface. The true magic of gaffer tape lies in its adaptability, its ability to seamlessly integrate itself into various aspects of our lives. Its enduring legacy is not confined to a particular application, but rather resides in its boundless potential. It's a material that transcends its simplicity, becoming a symbol of resourcefulness, creativity, and problem-solving.

So, as we bid adieu (for now) to this remarkable adhesive, let's not forget its underlying message: that sometimes, the most ordinary things can hold extraordinary power. The next time you reach for a roll, remember the journey we've taken together – from the factory floor to the movie set, from the artist's studio to your own toolbox. And remember, the possibilities are truly limitless. The sticky adventure continues… and it's up to you to write the next chapter. Happy taping!

APPENDIX

This appendix contains supplementary material, including a detailed breakdown of gaffer tape's chemical composition (for those with a penchant for minutiae), a gallery of further examples of gaffer tape's surprising appearances in film and television, and a selection of user-submitted "Uses" entries that didn't quite make the cut (though some are truly contenders for the next edition). You'll also find high-resolution images of Maurizio Cattelan's banana art (for those who prefer to examine it up close and personal, digitally speaking).

Actually, none of these things are included. They were there but, sadly, they were only held on by parcel tape.

REFERENCES

This book draws upon a vast and varied range of sources, from academic texts on adhesive technology to internet forums dedicated to DIY projects (and some truly bizarre YouTube videos). Specific citations would be unnecessarily distracting, but rest assured, my claims are (mostly) accurate. For truly rigorous research, I recommend consulting a qualified adhesive specialist —or just Googling "gaffer tape."

GLOSSARY

Gaffer Tape: A strong, pressure-sensitive adhesive tape commonly used in theatre, film, and television production, known for its ability to hold things together (and not leave a sticky residue).

Duct Tape: A close cousin to gaffer tape, often mistaken for its more refined relative but distinctly lacking in the finesse department.

Trenna Hoitytoit: A fictional, highly pretentious art critic whose pronouncements are best taken with a grain of salt (and possibly a roll of gaffer tape for emergency repairs).

Barry the White-Van Man: A fictional expert (of sorts) on all things adhesive, known for his unconventional techniques and questionable advice.

Maurizio Cattelan (Real): A real-life Italian artist known for his controversial and often provocative work.

Banana (Art): A banana, cleverly attached to a wall with gaffer tape, transformed into a multi-million-dollar piece of contemporary art (or a really expensive snack, depending on your perspective).

James Allen (author): is a humorous non-fiction writer and pop culture enthusiast with an unhealthy obsession with gaffer tape (a condition only exacerbated by the writing of this book). His other works (in production) include *The Surprisingly Deep History of the Paperclip* and *A Philosophical Examination of the Humble Spork*. When not exploring the world of adhesives, he can be found attempting to recreate Maurizio Cattelan's artwork (using slightly less expensive bananas).

ACKNOWLEDGEMENT

First and foremost, I must thank the humble roll of gaffer tape itself. Without its unwavering adhesive properties and surprising versatility, this book would have been…well, let's just say a lot less sticky. My deepest gratitude also goes to Maurizio Cattelan, for providing the artistic inspiration (and the banana).

To Trenna Hoitytoit and Barry the White-Van Man: your contributions, though wildly different in tone and approach, were equally invaluable (especially Barry's insights on wall adhesion).

A big thank you to my editor, whose patience was tested more thoroughly than the tensile strength of gaffer tape itself. Finally, thanks to all those who unwittingly provided gaffer-tape-related anecdotes throughout the years—your contributions, even if unintentional, are greatly appreciated.

ABOUT THE AUTHOR

James Allen

James Allen writes for fun - his, yours, everyone's. He uses the quirks and nonsense of AI generation to pay tongue-in-cheek homage to brilliant things that he thinks need more appreciation. His books are popular gifts and novelty items for those who want something light-hearted, funny, and seriously silly.

Printed in Great Britain
by Amazon